ALSO BY DONNA RUCINSKI

Math Myths for the Modern Child, Volume 1

Math Myths for the Modern Child, Volume 10

Call Me Edmund

Family Room Family

Coming soon: How to Buy Without a Realtor

REAL ESTATE WITHOUT REALTORS

Save Money Buying or Selling Real Estate

DONNA RUCINSKI

While care was taken in the writing of this book to provide up-to-date, complete and accurate information on real estate to homeowners and buyers at the time of publication, there may be errors, omissions or information that since publication has become outdated. The author is not providing legal or other professional services and there is no implied warranty of any kind. The author assumes no responsibility for errors, inaccuracies, omissions, or any other inconsistencies herein and hereby disclaims any liability to any party for any loss, damage, or disruption caused by errors or omissions, or any other cause.

ISBN 978-1-940507-15-6

Interior Images: Pixabay.com

Created with Vellum

FROM THE READERS OF REAL ESTATE WITHOUT REALTORS

Selling your home without a realtor can be intimidating! *Real Estate Without Realtors* showed me that it doesn't need to be. Using Donna's helpful tips, I confidently listed my home for sale by owner and I can proudly say I sold my house within a day and received well over asking.

— LISA

Real Estate Without Realtors gave us confidence to tackle selling a house ourselves. We learned to tell the story of our house in the listing and that, by taking a small step at a time, the process is manageable and, ultimately, pleasurable! We were amazed at the price we were offered and the tens-of-thousands we saved by selling ourselves.

— STEVE AND RHONDA

Buying without a realtor gave me the opportunity to own my own home for the first time.

— SOPHIE

I was hesitant to try FSBO, but Donna's knowledge and real-life experiences gave me the confidence to try. Learning about her many successes as a buyer and a seller, *Real Estate without Realtors* helped me work through every step of the process. I didn't know that I could hire a real estate attorney to represent me! It made all the difference in putting me at ease throughout the sale. With her help, my condo sold quickly AND at full price. This book is really useful for a new For Sale By Owner.

— SUE

Though I've been a For Sale By Owner in the past, *Real Estate without Realtors* gave me current advice for how to structure and word my home description and listing to be most attractive to buyers, and to reach them directly.

— THERESE

CONTENTS

Preface	xiii
Introduction	xv
1. HOW AND WHY	1
Why Do For Sale By Owner	1
How and Why I Got Started	4
How to Find the Information You Need in This Book	8
Chapter 1 Bottom Line	9
2. A HOME PURCHASED AT AUCTION	11
My First Purchase: Buying Through a Real Estate Auction	11
Using Gifts for Down Payments	12
Attending a Real Estate Auction	13
My First Sale: Easier Than I Thought!	15
Finding a Lawyer and the Logistics of Selling	15
Open Houses for For Sale By Owners	17
My First Open House	18
Chapter 2 Bottom Line	19
3. BUILDING A HOME	22
My Second Purchase: Building a Home	22
Construction Loans	24
Save Money by Doing Work Yourself	24
My Second Sale	26
Browsing Real Estate in Newspapers, and Realtors Commission Sharing	27
The Flexibility of FSBO	28
Chapter 3 Bottom Line	29

4. A HOME FOR EXTENDED FAMILY 31
My Third Purchase: Designing and Building a Home for Extended Family 31
My Third Sale: Does an Expensive Property Require Working with a Realtor? 34
After the Realtor: For Sale By Owner, Using the Internet 35
Allow Buyers in As Soon As Possible 36
Finding the Right Price Point 37
Factors to Consider When Deciding to Accept an Offer 37
Remember: The House Isn't Sold Until Closing! 38
How Much Earnest Money to Require with Purchase and Sale 39
Recovering a Deal When a Buyer Wants to Cancel 40
Problems with Buyers Happen With and Without Realtors 41
Problems with a Home Must Be Disclosed 41
Preemptively Check for Problems to Avoid Surprises 42
Chapter 4 Bottom Line 43

5. A MODULAR HOME 46
My Fourth Purchase: Building a Modular House 46
Using and Staging a Home For Family Life 47
My Fourth Sale 48
Be Wary of a Realtor's Offer to do a Comparative Market Analysis 50
Deciding on a Listing Price — Important! 52
Best Times to List 55
Do Owners who Do For Sale By Owner Fail? 55
Can a Realtor Get More for Your Home? 56
What You Should Know If You Can't Do FSBO 57
Know Exactly What Services Your Realtor is Going to Provide (or Not) 62
Avoid the Flat Fee Broker and the MLS (Important!) 63
Preparing Information to List Online 72
Offering a Co-Broke Fee to Realtors 73

The Most Important Marketing after Pictures: Your House Description 76
Carefully Craft Your House Description 79
Doing Research on Writing House Descriptions 79
Feeling Words to Use in Describing Your Home 83
Newly Written Ad Sells the Home 84
Offer Falls Through Due to Home Inspection Surprises 85
Disclosing Information About Home Problems 87
Hiring a Home Inspector to Avoid Surprises 88
View with Caution Realtor's Advice Against For Sale By Owner 88
Chapter 5 Bottom Line 91

6. BUYING WITHOUT A REALTOR - IMPORTANT ADVICE 95
Update in Response to the New Real Estate Commissions Rule, Enacted August 2024 95
Searching for a Realtor to Help with a Search 98
Email Notifications of Real Estate Listings — Not Enough! 99
How to Search Real Estate Without a Realtor 101
How to Deal With the Listing Agent Only 102
Bidding on a Bank-Owned Property 103
Making an Offer to the Listing Realtor After an Open House 104
Bidding Wars 105
Submitting a Well-Written Letter With Your Offer 106
How to Save When Buying: Search for For Sale By Owner Homes Specifically 108
Why You'll Save with For Sale By Owner 109
When to Consider Hiring a Lawyer 110
Negotiating Commissions 111
Negotiating a Lower Commission with For Sale By Owner 111
Remember, the Listing Broker is Working for the Seller 113
First-Time Buyer Savings 113
Chapter 6 Bottom Line 114

7. WHAT YOU SHOULD KNOW IF YOU USE A REALTOR TO BUY 117
Real Estate Browsing Was Once Only in a Realtor's Office 117
Realtors Became Experts in Their Region 117
All Real Estate is Now Viewable and Searchable Online 118
Real Estate Commissions and Who Pays 119
Make Sure Your Contract Doesn't Prohibit You from Buying Without a Realtor 120
When an Agent Might Not Be Acting in Your Best Interest 122
Chapter 7 Bottom Line 122

8. FOR SALE BY OWNER CHECKLIST 124
Step One: Hire a Real Estate Lawyer to Help You Navigate the Process 125
Step Two: Clean Out and Fix Up 128
Step Three: Hire a Real Estate Photographer, or Take Pictures 136
Step Four: Decide on a Price Based on Market Research or Hire an Appraiser 138
Step Five: Prepare Marketing Materials 146
Step Six: List Your House Online as For Sale By Owner 148
Step Seven: Schedule Open Houses on the Weekends by Thursday of Each Week 153
Step Eight: Submit Offers and Earnest Money to Your Attorney for Escrow, Sign P&S 158
Step Nine: Schedule an Inspection and Walk-through of your House 159
Step Ten: Prepare For and Attend Closing 160

Afterword 163
Thanks 167
About the Author 169

To my friend Therese Keohane
So much in common, but the most surprising:
Four times an FSBO!

So grateful for your friendship

PREFACE

Updates to this Book

I originally published this book in 2020, but I've come back to the manuscript to make a few updates.

The new Real Estate commissions rules that rolled out on August 17, 2024 has the potential to impact both buyers and sellers, and I wanted to address that for readers.

Primarily, I'd like to encourage buyers who, due to the new rules, may be unpleasantly surprised that they will be required to sign a contract, a buyer's agreement, before they are shown any homes (to insure their agent will be compensated) and could be expected to pay the commission for their (buyer's) real estate agent. Having to pay for a service that used to be payed by the seller, but free to them, they may want to consider buying without a realtor to maximize the dollars spent on housing, rather than realtor's fees.

Though this book was primarily for people who wanted to sell their home without a realtor, I also have a chapter in this book on buying without a realtor, and I believe not only saved money but gained an advantage when buying when I came to the table without a realtor representing me.

And though I'm planning on publishing a second book entirely focused on buying without a realtor, I'm starting by updating this book, so this book will also include updated information for both sides of the transaction.

I think the information is timely and very critical to buyers if their budget is so tight that they'd find it hard to pay their agent, and still afford the home they desire, and I'd like to offer some guidance on entering into contracts if you do decide to use a buyer's real estate agent.

Another update for this manuscript is to address the change Zillow has made to For Sale By Owner listings (they are now under a separate tab), which changes how I would recommend a seller list their home on Zillow, and in the MLS. Also, the new real estate commissions rule affects how sellers will want to think about offering compensation to a buyer's realtor.

I'm not a realtor, but have a lifetime of experience buying and selling without a realtor, and I've learned a lot of hard lessons. I think my stories will help others to hang onto their equity, and maximize their buying power. Though I still haven't recovered the costs of self-publishing, I know I've helped several people to navigate real estate without realtors a little more confidently, and I'm happy that this information saved them a lot of money.

If this book helps you, please consider leaving a review, as that will help make the book more discoverable to others, and recommend this book to others who are thinking of buying or selling, so they can save money, too.

Thank you, and good luck!

INTRODUCTION

My Credentials

My interests as a young girl were: reading, biking, writing, climbing trees, crochet. But another stood out: real estate.

When I was a teen, I enjoyed reading the real estate section of the newspaper. So when I discovered I could take a real estate class as an elective in college, I happily enrolled. The class was easy and it simplified real estate concepts to the point where I didn't see any reason why I shouldn't try selling my homes as a For Sale By Owner (also known by the acronym FSBO, pronounced here as fizz-bo). Eventually I would buy one home, build three, and sell each of them without a realtor. Assuming a 5% realtor's fee on each, I've saved approximately $68,740 throughout my lifetime of selling my own homes. That's a healthy chunk of nest egg that I could keep and use to increase my buying power substantially when I bought subsequent homes.

Other books about For Sale By Owner teach how to sell without a realtor, but I've also *purchased* five homes without a realtor's help. The first was a real estate auction, I built the second, the third I bought by going directly to the seller's realtor, and two were condos purchased without a real estate agent working on my behalf. Though at the time this didn't save *me* realtor's fees (because they were paid by the seller), in a competitive seller's market I believe it gave me an advantage in being the "winning bidder" on the homes.

However, with the new real estate commissions rules that went into effect on August 17, 2024, it's possible that some buyers will now be responsible for half of the realtor's commission. Though in the past a buyer hasn't had to pay to have a realtor represent them, show them homes, and help them with paperwork, that may not be the case when and if a seller refuses to pay for the buyer's relator.

My guess is this may motivate people to forgo the use of a realtor to help them purchase a home. They'll want to save those commission dollars to use on their downpayment, closing, or moving.

If you are buying and unsure of how to go about doing that, or know someone who is, please don't miss the chapter I've included on buying. Buying without a realtor saved me approximately $45,000.

I will be releasing a separate book strictly about buying without a real estate agent, but everything in that book will be included here as well.

There are so many scary articles out there that caution buyers and sellers of the dangers of buying or selling their home without a realtor, much of it written by realtors. But nothing bad has ever happened because I didn't have an agent, and that *includes* a lower selling price. I've been able to navigate, with the help of a real estate lawyer, and saved my equity for my pocket or for a down payment on the next home. I hope I can show you how you can do the same.

My experiences are from Massachusetts. In the past, I started with tiny ads in the *Boston Globe* newspaper, but once things moved onto the internet I found out how to get my home into the MLS (the Multiple Listing Service) and onto sites like Zillow.-com. Though my transactions were all in Massachusetts, most of my advice applies no matter where you live.

Though I earned an "A" in that real estate course in college, I never applied for my license or became an agent. I'm a layperson who has learned to buy and sell houses on my own. The college course gave me the confidence to try, though it feels intimidating at first. Once I sold my first house on my own, it was hard to see why I needed a realtor for any future sales, and that sentiment is shared by anyone who's done For Sale By Owner, they are satisfied with the process, because it works. Most people think selling a house is hard and complicated, but it's more tedious than difficult.

It's lucrative to sell your house on your own! And through experience I've learned how to navigate a FSBO safely and effectively. I wanted to share what worked, and what I learned from my many mistakes.

This book contains the information, advice, and stories I offer when friends ask for advice on navigating real estate purchases or sales without a realtor, but in much greater detail. I've helped five friends sell their homes without a realtor and another to purchase without a realtor. The book's an anecdotal account of my experiences, what each purchase or sale taught me, as well as safety tips, advice, and a to-do list, and critical information on how to advertise your home online so buyers can find you. It's a short book, meant to be a quick read and give you money-saving information you should know whether you are buying or selling a home.

In the first chapter, I'll show you how to navigate this book to find information quickly, and get on to buying or selling!

Chapter One

HOW AND WHY

WHY DO FOR SALE BY OWNER

Why should you buy or sell without a realtor?

The first and most obvious reason is that you'll save thousands of dollars. And if you are buying again, that money will increase your buying power on the next house. But there are other reasons you might prefer to buy or sell without a realtor:

- You have complete control over the process of selling.
- You are the one who arranges showings around *your* schedule and set the time for open houses (which can be as long and as frequent as you want them to be).
- You decide when the house is ready to go on the market, and if you need more time, you take it.
- You are the expert on your house, so you are the best person to market it. You know about the schools, the

neighborhood, what makes your town, neighborhood, and home special, and you know the most about improvements you've made to the home.

- A real estate attorney guides you through the process instead of a realtor providing expertise. They have deep knowledge of laws and requirements, having had more education than a real estate agent. A real estate attorney has a more comprehensive and in-depth knowledge than a realtor about the field, forms, process, and the law. Paying an attorney to handle the logistics of your home sale costs just a fraction of a realtor's fee.
- Though the realtor's fees as a percentage of the house sale seems small — 3-6%, as a percentage of the *equity* in the home, they're a much larger share of that, one that buyers may want or need to keep for themselves.
- Buying without a realtor can help you when there's more than one buyer trying to get the home. The seller's agent doubles their commission because they won't have to share half with your real estate agent, or, the seller may decide to offer to pay your realtor, which is a change with the new real estate commissions rule rolled out on 8/2024. If the seller doesn't have to pay an agent on your behalf, the net of your offer is more appealing to them.
- When you deal directly with the owner of a property, they have much more negotiation room on selling price because they won't have to pay your real estate agent a commission. If you like, a lawyer can double-check contracts for you for a reasonable fee.

If you search the internet for advice on being a For Sale By Owner, or on trying to buy without a realtor to represent you, there's a ton of ominous and disparaging advice. Most of it was written by people who have a vested interest in real estate transactions being handled by realtors. But it's not nearly as complicated to sell without a realtor as people think, or to buy without one, either.

There's a lot of new vocabulary, but you can get help with that (with this book, or the help of an attorney you hire) and be one of the roughly 10% (or more) of homeowners who sell without a realtor and save money. People who have done FSBO once usually gain the confidence to do it again. I've never talked to anyone who's done For Sale By Owner and regretted it, thought it was overwhelmingly hard, or thought that if it comes time to sell again, they would hire a realtor.

That's pretty convincing. If you need more reassurance, check out Reddit and read posts on the FSBO subreddit, you'll find some support there that is not influenced by realtors, and perhaps reading some success stories will encourage you to give it a try.

Most people suspect that selling a house themselves as a FSBO is very time-consuming, saying, "I'm busy, I can't possibly do that, I have to hire a realtor!" Perhaps preparing the home for sale and moving is overwhelming them, because *marketing* a house is pretty quick and straightforward with online tools, and comparatively, *not* time-consuming. I estimate that my last home took around 20 hours, total, to sell. That doesn't include getting the house ready to sell, or cleaning for open houses, because you have to do that *even if you hire a realtor*. Instead, it is the work that a realtor would have done, including doing research to price my home correctly, writing my ad, filling out forms online with information about my home, fielding calls, and holding open houses and showings. If I had paid a realtor to market the home, I would have saved myself being present for the open houses and showings, but I would have had to go somewhere for those hours. Instead, I was happy to be there, because for that 20 hours of rather pleasant work (compared to packing, staging, landscaping and cleaning), I saved many tens of thousands of dollars.

With a lawyer I hired to help navigate the process, I felt confident in my ability to do it correctly.

Moving is a lot of work, one of life's most stressful events. I wish you all the best whether you are trying to buy or sell a home. It's a uniquely personal purchase, involving all the "feels" that the word home elicits: shelter, warmth, safety, comfort, memories, family, pets, hobbies, and love. It's not just your biggest financial purchase, it's your biggest *emotional* purchase.

But, in the end, buying or selling real estate is a business transaction. My intention is to have my advice steer you effectively in that arena and save you money while preserving the pleasurable feelings and memories of your home ownership. I hope that by smoothing out the process I can help you avoid some stress, maintain the excitement of a big life transition, allow you to keep your equity, and empower you to find a new home you love for the right price.

HOW AND WHY I GOT STARTED

When I was a young girl I lay on my belly on the living room rug with the Sunday real estate pages spread before me, eating my Dunkin' Donut. Our living room held an odd collection of furniture my mother had bought at yard sales or from the *WantAd* (a pre-internet paper catalogue listing used merchandise for sale). The bought-on-sale carpet I lay on didn't match the furniture, but was cheap and going to last a long while, as the dining and living rooms were off-limits to everyday use.

My parents worked hard for never-enough paychecks and scrimped. My dad closely tracked gas mileage and fixed our cars; my mom bought used and cheap furnishings, bought day-old baked goods, knitted our mittens, and sewed clothes for us. But when it came time to sell the family home, my mother payed a realtor thousands of dollars, spending a sizable chunk of the equity in their home, which made up much of their life savings.

Even at age 12, I felt confident that real estate in Massachusetts was a good investment and would increase in value. I loved deciphering the concise descriptions of homes for sale:

3BR RNCH .25AC FPL OH1-3 100K

Which meant: 3 bedroom ranch on a 1/4 acre, fireplace, open house 1:00-3:00, $100,000

4BR COL 1AC GAR FML DR, CLDSC 225K

Which meant: 4 bedroom colonial on 1 acre, garage, formal dining room, cul-de-sac, $225,000

I was right about real estate increasing in value. The first home I bought has increased in value by over 700% in the last 35 years. Real estate would have been an excellent investment even if one paid cash for the properties, never mind leveraging the bank's money, substantially increasing return on investment. And keeping all the equity for yourself, instead of paying a realtor a commission, means the return on your investment is much larger.

As an example, when I bought my first house for $50,000 right out of college, I put down a $5,000 down payment (much of which I borrowed from my parents). When I sold it two years later for $100,000 (it was the 80s and real estate was going nuts), had I paid cash I would have realized a 100% return on my investment, and doubled my money over two years. But since I had only put down $5,000, my return on investment was 1000%. I got my money back 10 times (after paying off my mortgage). *And* I got to live there!

As a teen, I tried to convince my dad it was smart to invest in real estate and leverage the bank's money. He had limited savings. He was getting decent interest compared with today on his savings account balance, about 5%. But, since inflation was over 4%, the net result is that his money was barely earning anything.

I told my dad that a local city had inexpensive properties he could buy and rent out. But he grew up during the Great Depression, was fiscally conservative, careful and fearful with his money. He was obsessed with saving and keeping his money safe.

I don't just mean saving money by putting it in the bank; he wanted to save money on everything. He'd even put his glass with used ice cubes in the freezer for re-use when he had another soda! His stinginess alternately amused and frustrated us. He was an early adopter of "reduce, reuse, recycle," though his motivation stemmed from painful memories of the Depression, not concern for the planet. He wouldn't move his money out of an insured bank account to invest in real estate without lots of convincing, so I kept trying. Maybe I wanted to make up for being a daydreamy girl who often forgot to turn off lights, and whose use of a hairdryer, judging by my dad's reaction, seem to be costing him thousands each month in electric bills.

It was hard to find a property to buy - even 45 years ago - for the amount he had in savings, about $15,000, but I finally found one. It was a gingerbread colonial on the banks of a river. I showed my dad the ad, and was amazed when he agreed to go see it with me. He called the realtor and set up an appointment.

I couldn't believe how cheap it was or how cute it looked when we drove up. The dirt road we'd turned onto followed a river and had a few cottages along it, surrounded by woods. The house for sale was two stories tall with curly garnishes in the peaks, and siding that had scallops and zig-zags painted contrasting colors, a style known as a Painted Lady Victorian. I loved it on sight. We entered the kitchen, looked up at the lovely ten-foot ceilings… and then noticed the water stain all around at the eight-foot mark! I asked if the river water had really come in nearly to the ceiling, and the realtor casually admitted that "Yes, this house has occasional flooding," like it was no big deal. My dad rolled his eyes at me, and I gave up on trying to find a property for my dad to invest in.

But my passion and interest in real estate did not wane, and in college I was excited that a real estate course was offered as an elective. It was taught by a broker from a local realty company and I loved the class. I could have taken my real estate license test at the end of the semester, but didn't bother. I wasn't looking to be a realtor; my degree was in computer science.

But the real estate course helped grow my confidence as I learned about laws, procedures, paperwork, deeds, liens, financing, and commissions. I understood it, and was ready to buy. Renting seemed like a waste of money to me when I could instead pay off a mortgage and build equity, so I hoped to save a down payment soon and buy quickly. Though I never convinced my dad to buy, in my first chapter I'll tell you how I purchased a home as soon as I got out of college (hint: Dad helped then, but there are programs now for 1st time home buyers. Talk to a mortgage specialist — there's more about that in Chapter 6).

HOW TO FIND THE INFORMATION YOU NEED IN THIS BOOK

Moving is hard, both physically and emotionally, whether or not you use a realtor. Preparing a home for sale is exhausting and time-consuming. You have my sympathy, believe me. For those who are reading this book while getting ready to sell their house, I want to make it easy for you to read only the important bits and get started by summarize information at the end of each chapter . The details of each sale are here to show you that I come by my information through experience, and include both my successes and stories of my mistakes.

To quickly give you an idea of what's involved with FSBO, you can start by reading the Bottom Line summaries in each chapter, then go back and read more deeply about subjects where you need more information. I've listed actions step-by-step to break it down, so it's less intimidating for you, and to empower you to give selling on your own a try.

The book is laid out this way:

Chapters 2, 3 and 4: These chapters describe my past For Sale By Owner real estate transactions, the first three homes I sold. I include some cautionary tales and descriptions of what was easier back then and what was harder, things that went wrong and how I recovered from them, and when the real estate agent's job's completed. If you don't want to read these war stories, just check out the summaries, the "Bottom Line," at the end of each chapter for the important lessons in that chapter.

If you are in a hurry and want to get going as a FSBO, or are still deciding if it's even something you want to tackle, just go to Chapter 5, which describes my most recent sale, offers current advice and cautionary stories, and helps with deciding on whether or not to use a realtor. I've added new advice for hiring a realtor in light of the new real estate commission laws. Chapter 8 contains the "How to Do For Sale by Owner Checklist" of everything I would tell a friend who wanted to follow in my footsteps. If you're in a super big hurry, just start by reading the Chapter 8 checklist.

If you are looking to save money *buying* a home, Chapter 6 contains tips on saving money, cautions on that end of the transaction, and some advice for a first-time home buyer, and talks about the changes in the real estate world with the new real estate commission rules rolled out in 2024. Now that realtors are asking people to sign contracts before seeing homes, and are looking to guarantee they get paid, more buyers are considering buying without a realtor, and I hope this book can give those people guidance. It absolutely can be done, as my stories have shown.

CHAPTER 1 BOTTOM LINE

- Real estate transactions are less complicated than most people think, and knowledge about them is empowering for the layperson. **Hiring a real estate attorney will take care of any lack of knowledge and save thousands over a realtor's fees.**

- The hours a seller will spend marketing their home, which is all you are paying a realtor to do, aren't nearly as many as people expect, my last home was about 20 hours of work.
- As a For Sale By Owner, you have control over the entire process.
- Buying without a realtor can give you an advantage over other competing buyers.
- I have a lifetime interest in real estate and as a lay person have experience selling four homes For Sale By Owner, otherwise known as FSBO, and also buying four without a realtor.
- When buying real estate, you're leveraging the bank's money to get a return on your investment, and you get to live in that investment while you do so instead of throwing money away on rent. Most likely, your mortgage and taxes will be less than renting, but even if it's more, you're building equity as you pay down your loan, equity you will get back when you sell as long as the real estate market holds steady or goes up.
- Buying without a realtor may give you an advantage in a competitive market. Now that buyers are expected to guarantee their realtor gets paid, possibly by the *buyer* with money they hoped to use for the purchase, buying without a realtor is looking more appealing. Stories of how I navigate that process can help guide buyers.
- Selling For Sale By Owner allows you to keep a much larger chunk of your equity, increasing your return on investment and your buying power for your next home.

Chapter Two

A HOME PURCHASED AT AUCTION

MY FIRST PURCHASE: BUYING THROUGH A REAL ESTATE AUCTION

When I graduated college, I was eager to invest in real estate. Instead of spending money on rent, I wanted to put that money toward a mortgage for the purchase of my own home. I was married, and my husband and I went to visit some friends who'd purchased a house in our hometown. Their neighborhood was full of identical ranch homes on quarter-acre lots, built as housing for the soldiers of a local army base back in the 1950s. Down the street from our friend's house sat an identical home, except this one was obviously uninhabited; the windows were dark every night; the yard overgrown. Armed with real estate knowledge and confidence from my college class, I went to the local registry of deeds and looked up the records to see who owned it. We can now search this online, but back then you had to go to the registry in person, in the basement of the enormous court building in a local city. I discovered the house was owned by a bank, and when I contacted them I found out that the house was in foreclosure and going up for auction. I asked them about the requirements for bidding. My husband and I scrambled, talked to my dad about borrowing a portion of a down payment (we were just out of college and had no savings), and talked to a bank about getting financing.

USING GIFTS FOR DOWN PAYMENTS

Banks are sometimes okay with a down payment given to you, as long as you get a letter saying the money is a gift. If you have to pay it back, it's considered a debt that would affect your ability to pay your mortgage, like a car loan or credit card debt. Banks will only allow you to take on a certain percentage of debt compared to your income, known as the debt-to-income ratio. Typically, banks want 43% or less of your income to be for paying off debt, which includes the mortgage and all other loans, though some will let this go higher if your credit score is good. If you have a lot of debt like car loans, college loans, or credit card debt, these will count against you when you are trying to qualify for a mortgage. You need not go to a bank to get a rough estimate of what you can afford for a mortgage. Take 43% of your income, subtract out any loans, and the rest is what you can afford for your housing expenses, including mortgage, insurance, homeowner fees, and real estate taxes.

If you're lucky, a benefactor could loan you money for a down payment or pay down your debt, though check with the bank to see how they want that taken care of. Anyway, if you have a generous friend or relative who can help with a portion of a down payment, it's worth considering. I'll confess that the "gift" my dad gave us was, in reality, a loan. We planned to pay him back in full, and quickly.

ATTENDING A REAL ESTATE AUCTION

Today, buying homes at auction is a lot more common. But back then, this seemed like a crazy risky thing to do. The day of the auction came. I was excited to be investing in real estate, my dream since I was a kid, and with the prospect of having a home to live in with my husband. I still needed to win the auction, so I was also nervous. I didn't know if anyone else would show up at the auction, as the house looked pretty run-down from the outside, and we weren't allowed to enter it for inspection until the day of the auction. The real estate market was slow back then; today someone would snatch up a home like this in a minute. We'd snuck around the house in the previous weeks and peeked in the windows, getting excited when we saw that the house seemed to be in good shape. My husband's family was in construction, so we were confident that we could fix any problems we found when we got inside as long as we could purchase the home for a good price. We had a limit that we wouldn't go above, the only responsible way to enter an auction. We had a $5,000 deposit, and the bank required a 10% down payment for the mortgage, so $50,000 would be our top bid.

When we arrived at the house on the day of the auction, we finally got to tour the inside. Aside from some superficial damage and trash, it looked fine. Then we stood in the driveway where the auction was to take place. There was another couple, a man wearing a suit, and the lawyer who was the auctioneer. He started the bidding, not at zero, but, if I remember right, the starting number was the balance of the mortgage on the foreclosed property. We bid against the other couple for a few rounds, and the couple quickly dropped out, their upper limit apparently lower than ours. We were excited because it looked like we might get the house for $36,000. But then the man in the suit stepped in and bid up the house until we dropped out. We left the auction disappointed.

Turns out, that man was representing the bank, and the bank now officially owned the property. They called us up and offered the house to us at the amount of our last bid, which we happily accepted. We'd been so devastated when we didn't win the initial bidding war and figured we'd lost the house, so having a second chance to get into the house was amazing. I often wonder what would have happened had we dropped out of bidding before the $50,000. Would the bank have offered it to us at a lower price? But we didn't drop out sooner because we didn't know the man was from the bank; for all we knew, he was another buyer. Anyway, we had a home, and we were thrilled.

There are plenty of resources today to help you buy a house at auction, and my memory of this long-ago transaction shouldn't inform you on doing it today. But I bought my first house for $15,000 less than my friends bought theirs for. The information I had learned in my real estate course, along with my desire to own a home since reading the real estate pages as a teen, made me confident enough to try buying a home at auction. The company offering us a mortgage had an attorney working on their behalf, and part of that was making sure the property they were mortgaging had a clean title.

Real estate isn't as complicated as most people think, and for this first home, knowing a little about it made me feel comfortable jumping into a foreclosure auction.

MY FIRST SALE: EASIER THAN I THOUGHT!

Two years later, I was divorced and looking to move. Though I don't regret buying the house as an investment, I would advise against buying a house to save a failing marriage. We thought giving us something to work together on might help us, but it didn't work. On the bright side, I could sell the house for over $100,000, making a large profit. Again, this was the 1980s and prices were going through the roof. The only drawback to buying back then were the high mortgage interest rates. I believe my interest rate was 17% or 18%, as opposed to current rates, which are around 4%.

Because the market was so good I prepared to sell that house as a For Sale By Owner (FSBO). I felt confident that I could do so because my college real estate class was still fresh in my memory.

FINDING A LAWYER AND THE LOGISTICS OF SELLING

I found a lawyer — a friend of my brother's — with experience in real estate law who would handle the legal parts of the sale.

Before that could happen, though, each bidder would have to submit a standard "offer to purchase" form, offering to buy the house. Since it was soon after taking my real estate class, I had examples of standard offer forms, a document I would need all buyers to submit as the first step in buying my house. The "offer to purchase" form:

- Gives the price offered for the home
- Indicates the offer is contingent on a "satisfactory purchase and sale" document (a much longer

document outlining the sale with more detail to protect both the buyer and the seller)
- Is accompanied by a small deposit of "earnest" money — in this case, a $500 check made out to my lawyer

Once I had accepted an offer, my lawyer would take care of writing up the purchase and sale contract, which the buyer would sign (perhaps after running it by their own lawyer) and present with a bigger deposit, a percentage of the purchase price, usually 10 or 20%. My lawyer would escrow all deposits.

If the buyer walks away from the sale, the seller gets to keep the deposit for having missed time on the market when they might have sold to another party. It's devastating to the seller to have the sale fall through, and I've heard that some people have enough money that it's a strategy to give up their deposit if a home they like better comes along. So be cautious about reducing the down payment required for a deposit — that is a bit of insurance for you that your buyer won't easily walk away from the deal. Also, you'll need that deposit to pay the bills for owning the house for longer if they walk, especially if you have already made arrangements to live elsewhere.

With a lawyer on board and forms in hand, I printed off copies. I put a three-line ad in the *Boston Globe* real estate section, offering my house for $105,000. These are the important pieces of information I needed to fit into my ad:

- The acronym FSBO, signaling that I was selling my house on my own
- The address (just the street and number, as the ads were grouped under the town name together)

- My phone number (instead of the realtor's)
- A scheduled time for an open house (important!)

After including that information, I had so little space in that ad I may have only had room to say it was a 3-bedroom ranch. There were lots of acronyms used in those real estate ads, since you paid for each line, so sellers tried to convey the sense of a home in as little word count as possible, like:

3-BD RNCH .25 AC (three-bedroom ranch on a one-quarter-acre lot).

It was an art.

OPEN HOUSES FOR FOR SALE BY OWNERS

Some buyers feel nervous about talking to an owner and prefer having a realtor as a middleman in setting up appointments. An open house, though, is appealing to everyone (even, and often, people who have no interest in buying your house, but that's okay). The buyers can come look at the home without talking to the seller at all if they don't want to. Though an open house might not be the best way for a realtor to sell your home, I believe it's the best way for someone doing For Sale By Owner to sell a home. It's how I found all my buyers. People love to go to open houses and showing up for one is a low-pressure way to look at a house that's being sold by either a realtor or an owner.

Realtors don't really expect to sell homes at open houses; they usually use them to find more clients. If you go to a realtor's open house, expect to sign in with contact information and be asked lots of questions, like, "Are you working with a realtor?" "Do you have a home to sell?" "Would you like me to send you information on other similar homes that might interest you?"

"Where else are you looking?" "How soon are you looking to buy?" As you might guess, those questions have nothing to do with enticing you to buy the home where the open house is being held. The realtor is looking to recruit you as a client and be your buyer-broker. The conversation will mostly comprise questions like this, and then the realtor may point out the features of the house you are visiting, or allow you to tour it on your own. If you've hired a realtor to sell your house, it would be unusual for them to hold an open house every weekend; they've got other homes to sell as well. But as an FSBO, *you* can. Take advantage of that!

MY FIRST OPEN HOUSE

As soon as my first open house started, I had people pulling into my driveway, and I got a full-price offer before the end of the two-hour open house. It was a hot seller's market. The couple left a deposit check and signed the offer letter, right on the spot. I told them I would give the check to my lawyer to put in escrow and would give him the offer letter so he could write up the purchase and sale (P&S). I told them they should proceed with securing financing to buy the house and start the mortgage process. As the woman stood there holding a baby, I was excited to be moving on to building my next home, and happy that this young family would get theirs.

But keep in mind that deals sometimes fall through. The husband called me the next day and told me that after talking to the bank, they wouldn't qualify for the financing they needed to buy the house. Could he stop by that evening and pick up the check they'd left for the deposit?

Deposit checks don't get cashed by you and deposited into

your account; your lawyer puts it into an escrow account until closing. They make the checks out to your attorney. I hadn't yet turned the check over to the lawyer, so I said, sure, he could stop by that night after work.

He came in and we talked a bit about real estate, and I expressed my condolences that they wouldn't be able to buy the house. And then he tried to kiss me! I don't know what he was thinking, but I pushed him away, and he left. I'm sure I was polite in asking him to stop and to leave. I may have apologized that I didn't feel the same way, even. But I was alone in the house, confused, and just wanted him gone. I didn't know what this man was capable of, so I stayed courteous. I feel lucky that that's all that transpired.

I didn't worry about the sale falling through. I put another ad in the newspaper the very next Sunday and held another open house, this time with a friend on hand for safety. I found a new buyer right away — a chef, his wife and three kids — and this sale went through. My lawyer wrote up a P&S, their lawyer looked it over and approved it, and we all signed. The closing took place at the Registry of Deeds with myself, the family buying the house, and both of our lawyers. It cost me a few hundred dollars for my lawyer to handle the sale. I saved myself about $5,000 in real estate commissions on that first sale. As a young woman starting out on a career, I was grateful for these savings!

CHAPTER 2 BOTTOM LINE

- Putting money toward rent every month gives you a place to live, but putting money toward a house builds you equity in that house that you can recover later when you sell, if the real estate market holds steady or appreciates. Renting never provides a return for your monthly outlay. And a mortgage allows you to make the most of the appreciation of real estate by leveraging the bank's money.

- In a pinch, relatives can gift you money as a down payment, as long as they don't expect the money back. The bank will allow this with a gift letter and it can help you qualify for financing.
- You used to go in person to the Registry of Deeds to find out information like property ownership, sales prices, and liens, but now all that information is available online.
- In a hot real estate market, it's very easy to sell your house by yourself. I sold my first home in two weeks with a three-line ad, even after the first offer fell through.
- **Open houses are not how realtors usually sell homes (though it is an excellent way for them to find more clients). They are, however, a great tool for For Sale By Owner, a comfortable way for buyers to view your home, and you will probably hold more for your home than a realtor would, perhaps every week. You can also make individual appointments with people to see the home.**
- Hiring a lawyer to handle paperwork and answer questions (especially if you are new to real estate transactions) is essential and reassuring for both you and the buyer. It will be much less expensive than a realtor's fee. The lawyer can help you navigate the

offer letter, purchase and sale, and hold deposits in escrow, which will reassure your buyer.

- For safety, if you are selling on your own, consider having a friend be with you in your home when meeting with potential buyers. After the open house, meet in a public place.

Chapter Three

BUILDING A HOME

MY SECOND PURCHASE: BUILDING A HOME

With the profit from my first home — $50,000 in equity, earned simply because real estate appreciated so rapidly in the 1980s — I invested in my next project: building a home on land I bought from my parents.

They'd done the legal footwork to sub-divide the land and separate it into an acre for their house and a separate three-acre lot. They put an ad in the paper, and a builder offered them $25,000 for the lot. Being an avid reader of the real estate pages, I knew this was half the market value for a building lot in our town. My mother asked me to look at the purchase and sale document; because of the real estate class I took in college, I was the family expert. I read it carefully, and found out that the builder was offering to purchase the land at $25,000, but expected my *parents* would do the work required to get the lot approved as a building lot *before* they would pass papers and get their money. This was crazy; once the approvals were in place, the value of that building-approved lot was closer to $50,000. The builder was counting on my parents not knowing any better, locking in at a cheap price and making my parents do the work, spend the money, and shoulder all the risk that the land wouldn't turn out to be buildable. He would profit $25,000 just because my parents didn't know any better. Fortunately, I did.

There didn't seem to be any reason the lot couldn't have a house built on it. The only problem was some wetlands on the property, and it would require some applications and waiting for meetings of the planning board and the conservation commission in town. But with three acres, I was certain that there'd be enough dry land to allow for one house. So I offered to sell my home and buy the land at full market price if they allowed me to live at home while we went through the approval process together. I would then have a home built on the lot myself. My parents were fine with this, and I even paid rent to stay with them. I bought the land at the current market rate of a buildable lot, twice what the developer had offered. I was confident it would pass, they would get their money, and I would increase my real estate equity by building and doing some work on the home myself. Plus, I was excited about building a custom home. I started spending lots of time combing through magazines of home plans.

I was particularly interested in energy-efficient homes, but I couldn't afford custom built and had a hard time finding a builder willing to build just one custom house for me. It was hard to find a builder willing to take a young woman seriously. But a neighbor's son-in-law, though not willing to build me the home I'd fallen in love with in a magazine, would build me a house if I chose a plan from an architect that had archives of standard house plans. I was hopeful I could find something suitable in his collection, but when I went to the architect's house and looked through plans in his basement office, there was nothing like what I saw in my magazines. I went with a colonial that was a little less cookie-cutter than most, and I think I paid $100 for a copy of the plans. It wasn't my dream home, but I needed to get a home built, and this builder was the only one open to me at my price range.

Back then, the concept of an open kitchen/family room was new, but this plan had a big cathedral-ceiling family room off the kitchen. It was a two-story house with three bedrooms, two full baths, and formal living and dining rooms. I was to regret the formal spaces later and wished I'd built in more closets on the first floor.

CONSTRUCTION LOANS

When you are building your own house, either the builder finances it and you pay him when he's done, or you get a construction loan. The terms are different. While you are building, you pay all interest and no principal. My builder couldn't afford to take out the loan, so I did. When construction completed, the mortgage rolled over into a traditional mortgage.

SAVE MONEY BY DOING WORK YOURSELF

I did a lot to save money and get the most house I could afford, still looking to maximize my growing real estate equity. I bought a chain saw and my dad and I cleared the parts of the lot where the house would go. Fortunately, we had town sewer, and I didn't need to clear an additional space for a septic field. A long-time friend (my favorite customer when I worked my way through college waitressing) was a retired civil engineer and offered to come survey the land with me and stake the house location. I finally used my high school trigonometry as we tromped around the lot.

I tied ribbons around trees I wanted saved, much to my builder's annoyance, but I don't like it when builders clear-cut a house lot, leaving a house looking barren and lonely with no trees to tie a tire swing to, or to shade the house. I even cleared poison ivy off a tree, a big hairy vine that I pulled down and threw into a fire to burn leaves and debris. I roasted hot dogs over that fire and the next day I had to go to my doctor to get steroids for the terrible case of poison ivy rash I had all over my face!

The house building didn't go without a hitch, because the builder took my nice, loamy topsoil and spread it at his own new house. I questioned why it was being carted away, and he said that's how it was done, when my house was completed he'd be bringing that dirt back or the topsoil from the next house he'd build. Instead, I ended up with cheap fill that took years to get decent grass to grow in it. But overall, I had a new, solidly built house, three acres of land, and I hadn't had to put any more money down than what I sold my first house for. The land cost $50,000, and the house another $50,000, which was my mortgage. By the time I moved in, I was dating a man who would become my husband. He pitched in to finish the yard. I'd done a lot of the interior work myself already: installed a wood tile floor in the family room, put linoleum tiles in the bathroom and kitchen, painted most of the rooms, and installed light fixtures.

MY SECOND SALE

I lived in this house for about five years. I married that man who helped with the yard and we had a son. Six days after he was born, my dad died. My parents had still been living in the house I grew up in on the adjacent lot, which was easy to get to by walking through the woods on our property. I worked part time, and would drop my son off with my mom at my parent's house so she could babysit while I worked. My young family had a lot of memories, both good and bad, in that second house.

But not enough closet space. The formal living room and dining room didn't help at all when I needed space for a stroller, bouncy seat, portable crib, diapers, and wipes. A big pantry, or at least, another closet would have been more useful than formal spaces to entertain. It was nice, as a young working mother, to have a couple rooms that stayed clean, given that we hardly ever used them. But when company came, the family room opening off the kitchen was where everyone wanted to be. We never used the formal spaces.

After my dad died, my mom, my husband, and I started talking about selling both of our homes and buying another house, one with an in-law apartment. And more closets.

Eventually we did that. Same procedure as my first FSBO: I called the lawyer I used for my first house and told him I wanted to sell my second. I printed offer letters. It was 1993, and the market was not as hot as it had been when I sold before, but things were still moving. I was pregnant with our second child. My mother was excited about moving out of the old farmhouse where she'd raised her family, as it was too much for her to take care of on her own.

The logistics for the sale were the same as for the first house, as it was still before the time of the internet. We placed a three-line ad in the *Boston Globe* real estate pages every time we wanted to have an open house, using the acronym FSBO to identify us as For Sale By Owners.

BROWSING REAL ESTATE IN NEWSPAPERS, AND REALTORS COMMISSION SHARING

The real estate ads in the local papers were what buyers browsed before MLS (Multiple Listing Service) went online. The MLS was created when realtors would gather to talk about properties they had for sale with other realtors, and they would help each other, sharing commissions. For example, if a realtor agrees to list your home for a 6% commission, and another agent brings a buyer who purchases the home, they split the commission between the buyer's agent and yours. And some of each of those commissions go back to the broker, the person who owns the real estate agency that each realtor works through. In those days, the MLS meant that realtors had big notebooks that allowed you to see all the homes for sale in different towns. But they would also list a lot of these homes in the real estate ads, especially on Saturday and Sunday, so that was where many people started their search. If they answered a realtor's ad, they'd go to the realtor's office and see the listing sheet (a printed one-page description of the home with some pictures and a list of amenities and other details like real estate taxes). The realtor could then show them that home and offer to take them to similar homes that might interest them.

THE FLEXIBILITY OF FSBO

We cleaned like crazy, trying to make the house look perfect. We planted annual flowers on the walkway and put a fresh coat of paint on the front door.

With my young family, I could never live in constant "open house ready" mode. There were always some dishes out, laundry on the floor, or maybe the tub needed cleaning. So even though we weren't in a rush, selling added a burden to taking care of a toddler, a dog, a job, being pregnant, and the less-than-perfect level of housecleaning I usually aspire to. At least with being For Sale By Owner, we could determine when showings and open houses occurred, giving ourselves time to get ready. If we'd had a realtor, we'd have had to scramble whenever they found a buyer who wanted to look at our house.

We got a lot of calls on our ad from realtors who wanted to list our house. They can be very persistent. We held out, though their talk about selling the house quickly sometimes tempted us.

I don't remember that it took long to sell, though the sale wasn't as instantaneous as the first one. Maybe two or three months, which is about the average time to sell a house *whether you use a realtor or no*t. If you decide to be a FSBO, keep that in mind. As soon as you list, you are going to be anxious, wondering if you are doing the right thing, if it will every sell. You want to get on with your next purchase! But try to be patient for at least those three months that it would take with or without a realtor.

We had regular open houses and could afford to be patient, as we would move in with my mother while we found the next house. We wouldn't need to navigate buying another home right away.

A young man and his wife ultimately bought the house. He was looking for land on which to build a garage for storing big equipment, including a snowplow. The three acres gave him options for building a gigantic storage structure on the property.

The sale went smoothly, once again thanks to our attorney. Once we had an offer, the work went to my lawyer, who wrote up the purchase and sale (P&S) document. I believe I paid the lawyer $500 to represent us and handle the sale. Back then, we couldn't email, so we either mailed the documents or picked them up and delivered them in person. I gave the P&S to the prospective buyers, and they ran the document by their attorney, then signed. My lawyer held the deposits in escrow. We held the closing in the buyer's attorney's office. We sold that house for $193,000, getting a nearly double return for the original investment in the land and the building.

CHAPTER 3 BOTTOM LINE

- Read real estate contracts carefully or have a lawyer do so and explain the terms to you. Keep asking questions until you understand it fully.
- Building may require taking out a construction loan, where payments are interest-only until construction is finished, when the loan converts to a traditional mortgage.
- A clean, neat, uncluttered home is hard to maintain with a family, but it helps sell the house. Make sure your entry looks nice.
- A realtor can't help you with keeping a home show-ready, which I think is the very hardest part of selling.

- As a FSBO, you get to decide when you can be ready, and keep other times private.
- In a slower market it could take months to sell your home — on average, three months. *This is the same whether or not you have a realtor.* Be patient, don't panic, and don't believe realtors who try to blame it on the fact that you are For Sale By Owner.

Chapter Four

A HOME FOR EXTENDED FAMILY

MY THIRD PURCHASE: DESIGNING AND BUILDING A HOME FOR EXTENDED FAMILY

Though until now I hadn't even used a realtor to buy a house (first the purchase at auction, and then building on my parents' land), my family and I were now looking for a unique living situation: a house with an in-law apartment. There was nothing on the market; we felt certain we would need to build another home. We started looking at builders and their projects, housing developments where we could customize the home. My mother was particular; she required her own entrance and didn't want to live in a basement (which eliminates 99% of in-law apartments). But she would contribute to the construction of the in-law, and it made us happy to think of all of us living together.

We started working with a realtor who represented a builder of custom homes in a new neighborhood, but the builder ended up selling a lot we were interested in to another buyer. Perhaps it was because the other buyer was putting up a simple house, and we would require a lot of customization, given the in-law apartment. The realtor for the builder felt awful that he'd done this to us, so she worked at finding a consolation prize — a nice lot in a small, partially built, cul-de-sac project. She paired us with a different builder (her husband), and we started the part of the project that would be our home. At that point my mother would put her house on the market, finish the in-law, and move in. We lived with her after the sale of our house as we started building the new home, and my second child was born while we lived in the house I grew up in.

We built a four-bedroom house with an upstairs play room. Downstairs — besides the formal living and dining rooms (barely used again) — this time I was smart enough to add a mud room with two closets for coats. I also included a large walk-in pantry and laundry room right off the kitchen. The builder thought I was crazy as I moved walls to make the pantry as big as possible. In my head I had a lengthy list of the stuff I'd store in there: diapers, bouncy seat, portable crib, baby carriage.

I was learning how to design a house that worked, and that pantry was my favorite room. People would come over and say, "How is your house so clean?" If they were good friends I'd show them inside the pantry where, just before they'd arrived, I'd shoved all the clutter — laundry, toys, paperwork and projects, sometimes even a laundry basket filled with dirty dishes, which made the house look neat and made me look like I was efficient and in control, which I hardly ever was in those days. I showed people the mess-hiding pantry because I didn't want them to feel bad that somehow I was keeping up and they couldn't. We're all in this never-quite-caught-up game together; I'm was just better at hiding the evidence because of my big pantry. But hiding my mess made it so I had a clean kitchen tabletop where we could have tea and take a breather. I didn't care about my reputation of being a neat person (or I wouldn't have shown them inside the pantry) but I wanted to treat my friends to tea and a snack in a comfortable setting. I wanted it to be nice for them to come over. And that gave me a bit of a mental health break. Afterwards, well, all I had to do was tackle that mess in the pantry.

My mother had a wonderful in-law over the garage. She had her own staircase up from the garage, though most nights when she came home she stopped in to get a dose of grandchildren before she went up to her apartment. While living in that house we had two more kids, taking our total to four, making it so she could get a complete dose of grandchildren quickly. My husband did a lot of finish work on this house on some inside spaces and the yard. He did all the landscaping on the two-acre lot. I painted and wallpapered and sewed curtains.

We lived there for 10 years, and then the company my husband worked for announced it was going out of business. He'd also been talking for a while about wanting to move to a smaller town and trying to build his own home, a modular home. We purchased land one town over, in a small, very rural town with no businesses or services at all, though it was only 15 minutes to a city for shopping. We contacted the listing realtor for a woman who was selling her home and a parcel of 11 acres of land. We would buy her small cape home and live in it while we sub-divided and built on the land. At the last minute, though, she decided she wanted to keep the house. Her children convinced her to sell us the 11 acres of land. We agreed. My mother decided she wanted to move back to the town we grew up in, so she could qualify, after a year, for senior housing.

It seemed like a good plan to cash in on this house and use the money to build again.

MY THIRD SALE: DOES AN EXPENSIVE PROPERTY REQUIRE WORKING WITH A REALTOR?

When I talked about doing For Sale By Owner again, my friends, family and realtors tried to talk me out of it. They said, "Doing For Sale By Owner may have been okay for the homes you sold in the past, but at *this price point*, you need a realtor. People who have enough money to buy this house will want to deal with a realtor, a professional, not an owner."

Realtors also promised they would get more for my home because of all the ways they could market my high-end home. I fell for this line of reasoning, as the home was big and expensive, and I didn't want to mess things up because I was stubborn about being a For Sale By Owner. We asked a realtor to list the house for just over a million dollars.

We still had to prepare the house for sale, clean everything up, touch up paint, fix any problems, get rid of lots of belongings. It was a lot of work.

And then the house sat. It was still a ton of work to sell a home with a realtor, as by that time I had four children, and keeping a house ready for a showing with four children is nearly impossible. I couldn't shove the mess into the pantry like I did when friends came over, as prospective buyers would look into every closet, the basement, and the garage, too! There was no place to hide any mess. The house had to be spotless while a family of 6, plus my mother, lived there.

I remember a realtor calling at 7:30 at night and asking if she could show the house. I had the kids in the bath; the downstairs was a mess. But she pressured me into it, saying it was fine if I didn't want to show the house, but I would probably lose these buyers, as they were looking to decide soon. I had to grab kids out of the bath, get rid of dirty dishes, diapers, and laundry by putting it all in the back of my mini-van, buckle the damp kids in, and get out of the house. It was inconvenient and stressful.

AFTER THE REALTOR: FOR SALE BY OWNER, USING THE INTERNET

After six months and no offers, our realtor's contract expired. We immediately had offers from several other realtors (they must know the day that the contract with the realtor expires) promising they could do a better job to get the house sold. I decided to once again try For Sale By Owner, as having a realtor hadn't proved to be the trick to selling at this price point. And not only was I not sure a realtor could do a better job, but I was looking at saving commissions of anywhere from $40,000 to $60,000, which, given my husband's soon-to-be-unemployed status, was nothing to sneeze at. We could live on that for a while.

By the time I was looking to sell this third house, we had the internet, including a site called Forsalebyowner.com. I signed up at that site. I also paid a realtor a nominal fee to put the house into the Multiple Listing Service (the MLS, where most people look for homes), and the MLS was now searchable online. Back then, my house would show up as a "by owner" sale, and it listed my personal contact information. *This is not the case with the MLS today.*

It still took a few more months to sell. We still listed in the Sunday real estate pages for the open houses we scheduled ourselves on Sunday afternoons. Sometimes people feel uncomfortable dealing directly with an owner — though less every day as more people are trying the FSBO route, and both buyers and sellers are looking to save money. Perhaps buyers afraid of a hard sell, or having to insult your home to your face in negotiating a price. I found that having an open house was a way to give people a chance to see the house and fall in love with it, with no pressure. Check Chapter 8 on FSBO for more information about how to do this, including safety tips.

We created our own listing sheet with information and pictures from our ad, and gave this to prospective buyers. We included copies of the floor plans, which people loved. We had the full set of building plans available at the open house for buyers to inspect, as well as a landscape design.

ALLOW BUYERS IN AS SOON AS POSSIBLE

Having a home ready to show at all times with small children (I now had four) is impossible, unless you are a much more high-functioning human being than I am. Nowadays you can ask your realtor to put "24-hour notice before showing" in the listing. If you go with a realtor, I'd recommend this. If you are selling by yourself, you can negotiate showings right away if you are ready, or give yourself a day to shine things up. It's an excellent rule of thumb to let people see the house as soon as possible, as you don't want to give them time to fall in love with someone else's home. But unless the buyers are pressed for time, 24 hours is reasonable and gives you some time to prepare your home for the showing. If your house isn't perfect but the buyers really want to see it right away, give in to showing a less-than-perfect house. Just give them a head's up that it's not as neat as you would like it to be for a showing.

FINDING THE RIGHT PRICE POINT

Eventually a couple came to an open house and offered $895,000 for our home. Though this was below the original listed price, by this time we'd realized that we'd started too high when we listed with the realtor, and we accepted their offer. A realtor once told me, "Any house will sell, you just have to find the right price." When your price is low enough, your house will be a bargain to someone. To relieve ourselves of the stress of continuing to list, the uncertain nature of my husband's job, and the continued expenses of staying in this house, we accepted the offer and moved forward.

After this sale, because of the appreciation of the real estate, we would clear over $500,000, and have that money to purchase the land and build in the next town. We weren't even going to need a mortgage to do so. And thankfully, this couple had no realtor, either, so we would pay no one but our lawyer at closing.

FACTORS TO CONSIDER WHEN DECIDING TO ACCEPT AN OFFER

We knew that in accepting this lower offer we'd get selling over with, and my husband's employment was nearing an end, so saving the additional months of mortgage, utilities, and taxes we'd have to pay if we stayed longer hoping for a higher offer was appealing. Take financial factors like this into account as you are weighing offers that come in lower than you hoped. Again, being patient can sometimes pay off, though I'm sure, like me, you'll be wishing for a crystal ball when it comes time to decide in this situation. Also remember that what you hoped to get for the home might not reflect its market value. If you feel as if you might have overpriced your home, comb through the comparable sales again and make sure you are being realistic. See Chapter 8 for information on how to come up with a good asking price.

If you work with a realtor, you might find that realtors will encourage you to take a low offer. Getting $10,000 more for your home, which is significant for you, is only another $500 (depending on the commission percentage) for your realtor. And accepting the low offer means they've finished their work on your home. If you accept a low offer, the closing — and thus their paycheck — will come sooner.

REMEMBER: THE HOUSE ISN'T SOLD UNTIL CLOSING!

Though we finally had a solid offer, the sale wasn't smooth. Again, I hired a lawyer, and she was incredible. She charged one set price, $1500, for the entire process, not an hourly rate. And she was very knowledgeable, having been a realtor herself for 30 years prior to becoming a lawyer.

So we got ready to move. We decided, since my husband would soon be out of work, that we would take the kids on a cross-country trip for three months. We would move into a residential hotel for the last month of my husband's employment after the house closed. We put all our furniture and belongings in storage, doing the moving ourselves. It was an exhausting amount of work and we were looking forward to it being over.

In the meantime, the buyers were asking us to fix every minor thing. We had to paint ceilings, patch holes, replace light fixtures, finish up any unfinished home improvement projects. It was frustrating and time-consuming, but we didn't want this sale to fall through. We'd now had our home on the market for almost a year, which had been stressful. We always had to be ready to show the house and didn't know when it would be over.

In the weeks before closing, our buyers went strangely quiet. We were trying to schedule a walk-through (when the buyers get to do a last inspection of your home before closing), and our lawyer called theirs, trying to set up a time for this. They were not responding. They never did. We were waiting in a cafe for word on what was happening on the day of closing, when the lawyer called to tell us the buyers canceled it. They didn't want the home. I was furious. I had four kids, and now we had to move back into our empty home and try to sell again? I told my lawyer that I would keep their deposit for this inconvenience. It devastated us.

It turned out that the buyers had gone to the town hall on their own and found out that our home had a four-bedroom septic system, but with the in-law apartment, the home was a five-bedroom. This was the reason they pulled out of the sale. It shocked us as we were unaware we had this problem.

HOW MUCH EARNEST MONEY TO REQUIRE WITH PURCHASE AND SALE

It crushed us, but we had their deposit in escrow. I was glad that we had a 5% down payment and hadn't allowed for it to be lower. If I got to keep that deposit, I could pay bills for a few months until we found new buyers. My advice would be to make sure you get enough earnest money when you sign a purchase and sale to make it hard for buyers to walk away from that money and the agreement to purchase your home. My lawyer explained that if I could resolve the problem in 30 days, it would require them to buy the home; if they still refused, I could keep the deposit. If I couldn't resolve the problem, I'd have to return their deposit and find new buyers. She was doubtful I could pull it off, but determined, I began fixing the problem.

RECOVERING A DEAL WHEN A BUYER WANTS TO CANCEL

When we were building the house, we had asked the builder to slide the house forward on the lot to give us a larger back yard. Allowing for this required the installation of a complete back-up septic system in the front yard. I was told if the first system ever failed, all I had to do was punch out one pipe and we were all set. It was a selling point.

After the closing fell through, I went to the town hall where I was told that yes, the septic wasn't technically big enough, but it had been 10 years and that grandfathered it in, and the town wouldn't do anything about it. I communicated this back to the buyers through the lawyers, but they didn't want to accept this resolution, and they still wanted their escrowed deposit back. So, back to town hall where I explained that I wanted to punch out the backup septic system, and have a double system, essentially an eight-bedroom septic system. The town agreed this would be plenty to support the 5-bedroom home. Now I had to find someone willing to draw up plans and do the work within the 30-day timeframe. I was lucky and squeaked by in just enough time. The buyers bought a house with no backup septic system, but with a legally compliant and abundantly adequate system.

And we took our three-month road trip as planned, after spending another six weeks in the house eating off paper plates and sleeping on mattresses on the floor.

PROBLEMS WITH BUYERS HAPPEN WITH AND WITHOUT REALTORS

As I rushed around fixing our house so the buyers would follow through with the sale, we were living in a minimally furnished house; I was under pressure to complete the redesign of the septic in under 30 days; and because my husband was out of work, we worried that we wouldn't get this sale to go through. That would mean starting from scratch and moving our furniture back in. With no income, money would become an issue quickly.

Some friends who knew what we were going through would say, "Well, maybe if you'd had a realtor, this wouldn't have happened!" misunderstanding what a realtor's responsibilities are. If I had had a realtor, they may have tried to help get the deal back on track (though I can't think of what more they could've done that my lawyer, the buyer's lawyer, and I were already doing), because otherwise, they wouldn't get their commission. But this isn't the part of the deal a realtor handles, they are *marketing professionals*. A realtor might have wanted to put the house back on the market, not try re-designing the septic, figuring the best way to get their commission was to re-list, maybe even cut the price.

PROBLEMS WITH A HOME MUST BE DISCLOSED

If we had put the home back on the market, we would have had to list the home with a disclosure that the septic was undersized for the house and the in-law apartment, which would have made it harder to sell. If you know there's something wrong with your home, you must, legally, disclose it. Talk to your lawyer about disclosure documents and by all means, don't hide any problems with your home. We didn't realize the septic was undersized; we thought the builder would have been sure to leave an allowance for the in-law apartment because they roughed it in when we started the home. If there had been a lot of demand for our home, more buyers to choose from, we probably would have sold the house when the realtor had listed it. Maybe we would have felt we could walk away from these buyers when they didn't show up at closing, or even before that, as they had made many, many demands for repairs. But this market was slow, this was the only serious buyer we'd had, we'd waited over six months for a decent offer to come in, and my husband was soon to be out of work. So we made this deal work.

I would gently remind friends who tried to blame this difficulty on my being For Sale By Owner that I'd tried selling with a realtor for six months and that when your home is under agreement, the realtor has finished their job. I didn't really care whether my friends understood this, except that I knew they all had homes that would cost them a lot in real estate commissions if they sold with realtors. I wanted to explain to them that my problems had nothing to do with being For Sale By Owner so they would have the confidence to try FSBO themselves and save money. I've heard lots of scary buyer stories about other people who had buyers back out at the last moment, and all of those people had realtors. One doesn't relate to the other. This story could have happened to anyone, realtor or not. It is good to remember that it's not over until you have closed on the home. Only then can you breathe a sigh of relief.

PREEMPTIVELY CHECK FOR PROBLEMS TO AVOID SURPRISES

As an insurance against any surprises at the inspection or beyond, consider hiring a home inspector on your own before you list, so you know if there's something you need to fix or disclose. Their report can also be a selling point as you can offer it to prospective buyers so they feel better about the home.

CHAPTER 4 BOTTOM LINE

- Keeping equity when faced with a lay-off or other financial concerns can be crucial, so selling For Sale By Owner can be financially desirable, if not critical.
- Thoughtfully consider what you use the spaces in your home for. Design a home for everyday living or consider taking over formal spaces for everyday use, which might make your home more appealing to today's families. A craft/homework room instead of a dining room. A movie room instead of the formal living room.
- I hired a realtor because I was told that an expensive home would require it to appease the buyer, but the house did not sell in the six months I was under contract, and sold once I went back to FSBO.
- People will try to talk you out of trying For Sale By Owner for high-end homes, but consider the alternative: spending a larger portion of your equity. The way percentages work means the savings on high-end homes for doing FSBO can be tens of thousands. Why not try it? You can always hire a realtor after. Or try using a realtor for a shorter time - six weeks or three months. Six months is a long time to commit to something, especially if it isn't going well.

- The hard part of selling a home has nothing to do with being For Sale By Owner, and it's nothing that a realtor can help with. It's cleaning, fixing up and preparing a home for selling, and then vacating the home when a showing will happen, especially if you have a family. Having control over who sees the house when is an enormous benefit of being FSBO and helps you work around family life.
- When someone backs out of a purchase and sale unless they have a good reason, you can keep their deposit. Be cautious then, about accepting a lower deposit than normal; it reduces both the buyer's incentive to complete the purchase and your compensation should the buyer walk away. Your purchase and sale document should give you the option of fixing lower-cost problems instead of returning the deposit if you decide it's worth it to do so. Make sure your lawyer puts that into the paperwork.
- Consider paying for a home inspection before you list, which will alert you to any problems. The report can be a selling point for prospective buyers. If you know of or find problems with the home, those must be fixed or disclosed when listing.
- A realtor can negotiate problems that occur after signing purchase and sale, but in reality, at that point they've finished marketing your home. They might be happy to let a troubling buyer drop out and re-list the home, but consider how much harder it might be, especially if you then need to disclose undesirable information about the house. Consider the cost of

staying in the home if you were to re-list before deciding whether to back out of a deal (or let your buyers back out). Talk to your lawyer about helping with negotiations at this point if you don't have a realtor.

Chapter Five

A MODULAR HOME

MY FOURTH PURCHASE: BUILDING A MODULAR HOUSE

My family lived in an apartment for a long while after we sold our last house as my husband prepared to build a modular house on land we had purchased in a rural town. He learned how to design a modular home, then had it built and delivered in four modular pieces and set with a crane. He then worked with subcontractors or worked himself to connect the boxes, stitching together the walls, plumbing, electrical, and finishing the roof. It took almost two full years of apartment living to complete our house to a stage where we could move in, and it was still incomplete. We built the garage and two more bedrooms over it after we moved in, which took another year. We had two lots, and the plan was to build this practice house on the front lot that we'd live in while he built our dream home on a larger parcel out back.

So it took a while, but then we owned outright a four-bedroom house, partially because of the savings of doing work on it ourselves, but mainly because of the equity that had built up with previous real estate sales, much of which we'd conserved by doing For Sale By Owner.

USING AND STAGING A HOME FOR FAMILY LIFE

In a previous chapter, I finally learned what my family needed to be comfortable in a house. Instead of a formal living room, this modular house had a walk-in pantry, an entry hall with a cleaning closet, a big mud room with a bench and coat hooks, and a gear room for winter coats, camping supplies, and an upright freezer. I furnished the "dining room" with home office furniture instead of a dining room set, giving us a terrific space for computer work, craft projects, paperwork, or homework. The piano was in there also, across the house from the family room so the piano wouldn't drown out TV watching. I mention this because when you are staging (or living in) your own home, consider setting up spaces in ways that will best serve yourself and/or your buyers. The work space instead of a formal dining room was appealing not only to me and my family, but I hoped to appeal to buyers who have families.

Our home sat on two acres, and had a three-car garage and an upstairs playroom, a rough-finished walk-out basement, granite and stainless steel kitchen, 2x6 construction (the walls were framed with 2x6's instead of 2x4's, providing more insulation), hardwood and tile floors, custom woodwork, a master bedroom suite, and walk-in closets. We owned another nine-acre parcel for the future house out back. Though this first modular had been the practice house, I had made sure I had input to the design, so I knew I could be happy living there if we never built the back house. It was a lovely, solid home, designed to make both family living and entertaining easy.

MY FOURTH SALE

I was glad I helped design our modular house, because I ended up living there for 10 years.

However, the stress of moving and building, living in an apartment for two years with a large family, unemployment, or perhaps something else entirely, were too much for the marriage to endure. After about five years in this house, we separated. When my youngest was in his last year of high school, the required (by the divorce settlement) upcoming sale was hanging over my head. I started cleaning out; all those big closets held sizable amounts of unnecessary items. I donated carload after carload to a local thrift store. I started reading articles on minimalism.

I tried desperately to get the things done that I felt I needed finishing to get the house on the market, the yard work being the worst of it. It was so stressful and time-consuming. I was a single working mom, and I hadn't kept the yard picture-perfect. Yard work wasn't high on my priority list, and I didn't even have the physical strength to do some of it. But I knew the first impression of a home is important. The yard needed to be neat and not look like a project the new owners would have to take on. There was an above-ground pool in the backyard with a broken liner that needed replacing. It was an eyesore and would be a big negative for the buyers. I couldn't remove the pool — without it, there was a wrap-around deck that would look strange. I couldn't replace a pool liner myself, so I called pool companies to replace it, and only found one willing to do the work — in 90 days! The front yard needed raking and re-seeding. The overgrown beds in front of the house contained bushes that needed clipping, weeding and mulching. The availability of landscapers to give an estimate that busy spring was near zero, never mind do the work. So I dug into that work with the help of my sons, but it was slow going. I raked, I weeded, I seeded, I fertilized, I watered, and when I wasn't doing that, I was cleaning out the house, painting, taking down family photos and art, making the house look generic, welcoming, spacious and empty.

People will say that the work you do to get your home ready for selling will make you want to stay in the home, as it will never look better!

It will also exhaust you.

Whether you do this with a realtor or without, this will be hard, and a realtor won't save you from the work of preparing, cleaning, and staging your home and yard, and then packing and moving. Make sure you have some support or at least factor in some self-care. You might be afraid to tackle For Sale By Owner if you are on your own, but I did it on my own, and frankly, the control I had over the process (when showings would be, and therefore, when the house had to be clean and tidy) more than outweighed having a realtor's help. I had my lawyer, a knowledgeable safeguard, and that helped me feel confident about going it alone. And if you are single, the money savings might be much more important to you than if you have a dual-income family.

The real estate market was hot and given my past successes there was no question I wanted to try For Sale By Owner again. I had experience doing so and was proud of this beautifully designed house. I expected it would sell quickly.

And if I couldn't get it sold quickly — even in this seller's market — I would seek a realtor's help. This is the advice I give most people who ask me about doing For Sale By Owner: Try it out for a few weeks or months (remember it takes on average 3 months to sell even with a realtor), and then if you don't have any luck, hire a realtor. Because of the divorce and the agreement that we would sell and split the proceeds of the house, selling the house quickly was a top priority for both myself and my ex-husband. We wanted to get on with our lives. My ex-husband agreed to allow me to do For Sale By Owner, as he'd been through it when we sold our last two homes, and he, too, was interested in maximizing the equity we kept in our pockets.

BE WARY OF A REALTOR'S OFFER TO DO A COMPARATIVE MARKET ANALYSIS

Despite my plan to do For Sale By Owner, when I was out looking at rental properties to move into after the sale, two realtors *insisted* on coming to look at my home. Inventory of homes for sale was low, and they were eager to get my listing. Though I was up front in my plan of selling on my own, I thought it wouldn't hurt to see if I could work with the realtor if I wasn't successful. I wanted to know if their plan to market my home was more than I could do myself, and to see the market analysis they offered for free.

When a realtor does a "Comparative Market Analysis," they'll tour and measure your home. They'll probably compliment your home, to show you they share your view of how unique and lovely it is, and that they will have no problem selling it. They might even say they have buyers already lined up looking for a home just like yours. Then they will go away for a day or two, while they generate the comparative market analysis booklet, and will ask to make an appointment with you to present the market analysis when they finish. They will want all decision makers present (owners of the house, so maybe you and your spouse) when they show you the market analysis so that there will be no delay in hiring them as your realtor. Having the decision makers present is usually a sign that you will get a hard sell and they'll want you to sign a contract to sell at that meeting. But it's your home and your decision. Take your time, even if it's just 24 hours to think it over. The contract you sign will be a binding legal agreement.

Two realtors did a market analysis of my home. I think realtors offer this free service not only to come up with a price for the home but also because they want you to feel obligated to hire them once they are nice enough to spend all that time generating the report for free.

To do a market analysis, the realtor will search for all the homes recently sold in your town — preferably close to your neighborhood — and also for homes currently on the market. They look for homes similar in size (square footage, calculated by multiplying the length times the width of every room, then added up together), in the number of bedrooms and bathrooms, and also similar in other features like garage size, master bedroom suite, lot size, etc. They generate a bound booklet with these home listings and data on each. Also included in this booklet will be the brokerage's marketing information, such as how broadly they can market your home, what their sales have been, and what they will do to market your home. It will be slick and have lots of colored pictures and graphs.

The reports are impressive. Since I'm a software engineer, I suspect much of the content of those reports gets generated automatically. It wouldn't be a hard thing to automate. But the realtor will imply it took lots of time and in-depth knowledge and experience to generate the report, and that it's reckless to dismiss this expertise and their company's breadth of marketing reach, only if you hire them will you reach amazing amounts of customers, and solely with their help can you ensure that only qualified buyers will look at your home.

"You don't want to be wasting your time with people who are just shopping for decorating ideas," you will be told. Also: "You need to pre-qualify buyers or you are wasting your time."

They may try to make you feel guilty for the time they spent generating the report. One realtor was so high pressure, she exclaimed, "I spent hours on that report!" while on the phone with me. The fact was, she had insisted on spending the hours, I hadn't asked her to do it. I heard her broker in the background feeding her more high-pressure sales lines to give me as I was telling her I would do For Sale By Owner and would not be needing her services. She even tried to schedule an open house without consulting me! I would never have hired this realtor after she treated me so disrespectfully. If she was hoping to be my backup realtor, she failed the screening test.

DECIDING ON A LISTING PRICE – IMPORTANT!

I thought I might get low-to-mid $600,000 for my home. The first realtor's market analysis gave me an estimate of $589,000. Another was non-committal, though, when I asked her point-blank if she could see me walking away with $600,000 plus her commission. If I hired her, she said she thought she could (though made no promises). I was still doubtful a realtor could do any more than I could.

I initially listed at $648,000. The realtors who spoke to me about listing my house would expect to make 5% of this sale. If I was lucky and sold the house myself at full price, I would save $32,400 in commissions.

Realtors most often split commissions between the listing (seller's) agent, and the agent who brings the buyer. Realtors love it when they both list a property and find a buyer because they get the full commission themselves. But often, they are only on one side of the transaction, and get half of the percentage. Some of that fee also goes back to the brokerage company they work for.

When I look at a real estate listing, I always notice not only the sale price but the house value estimate given by the listing site. Realtors will tell you those estimates are inaccurate and only a real market analysis of your home (done by a realtor) will give you a valid number, though I've found those numbers are usually on-target. In the course of listing my home's estimate on the site did vary wildly by tens of thousands of dollars at first, but then it seemed the software figured out where my house fit and settled on an accurate estimate. In the months before I listed I had regularly seen the Zillow.com estimate for my house hovering around $618,000, but just before I listed, it dropped to below $600,000. It would be bad for my ad if I listed my house way over what the site estimated. But I'd done my homework and my own market analysis (which I will teach you to do) so I knew I was in the right ballpark. The problem with some of these real estate web sites — especially for a tiny, non-homogeneous town like mine — is that it's very hard for them to find recent comparable house sales by which to judge the market value. The real estate site seemed to suffer from exactly this problem as its software struggled to price the home correctly. The drop was probably because of a recent sale that had some features in common with mine, but perhaps not a truly similar comparison. For example, perhaps a four-bedroom home with the same square footage sold recently, but it was an older home than mine so not a good comparison to my newer house.

Comparable homes, known as "comps" for short, are what realtors use to price your home. For mine, there weren't that many homes big enough, new enough, or custom enough to compare it to. My house, as a "builder's own" had lots of special features, and it was large. One buyer came in and said the home was ahead of the curve, that other builders were only recently starting to design "project rooms" instead of formal living spaces in the houses. I designed my house for a large family to live in comfortably, with space for everyone and all their hobbies and their stuff.

As soon as I listed my house the listing site's estimates shot up by $10,000, then $20,000, and the site's estimate was soon hovering right around my listing price. Magic, right? For this reason, I would be cautious in trusting those estimates completely. Realtors say this, too, because they believe that their method of finding comps and then adding and subtracting values of features to get the right pricing for your house is the only way to get a good estimate of market value. They may be right, or at least more right than the software on the real estate listing sites. But when it comes down to it, it's a matter of finding the right buyer for your home, and what they can afford and will pay. And this is variable. It relies on people's tastes and emotions and pocketbooks when they enter your home. And it needs to take into account not only the other homes on the market in your town, but often, what homes are going for in similar towns close to yours. You guess at it, but it's hard to quantify reliably. Still, you'll come up with a price that's as educated as a realtor's (I learned to do this when I took real estate licensing training), following the same methods. You'll be doing your own market research, and with online tools, it's easy. Thankfully, the days are gone when you had to go to the registry of deeds to gather the information. See Chapter 8 for more details on this, but it involves looking at recent home sales and the price per square foot of homes similar to yours. Or, you can also take a shortcut and pay a real estate appraiser for an accurate accounting of the home's current value.

BEST TIMES TO LIST

The biggest mistake I made selling my modular house was in not listing it in the spring. My house was a family house, and most families want to avoid moving while the kids are going to school, especially if it means moving to a new school district. And the real estate market was strong that spring. It slowed, but the realtors were saying the only reason for that was lack of inventory, so I still thought it poised me to sell fast. I finally listed in July, which wasn't ideal, as many people are away in summer or out enjoying good weather. The real estate market picks up again in the fall when people return from their summer vacations.

DO OWNERS WHO DO FOR SALE BY OWNER FAIL?

If you list your home in the MLS for a flat fee and sell, the NAR (National Association of Realtors) counts you as having sold with a realtor even though you are a For Sale By Owner. I sold my last two homes For Sale By Owner, but I listed both with a flat fee in MLS. I consider myself to be fully For Sale By Owner, but they misrepresent those two homes in For Sale By Owner statistics because of how the NAR interprets a flat-fee listing.

Realtors will try to convince you that most For Sale By Owners fail. An internet search will reveal that, unless you are looking at statistics presented by the NAR (National Association of Realtors), people who sell their home counts for 10% of home sales. But since this *doesn't include For Sale By Owner homes that listed as a flat-fee listing in MLS,* it could be as high as 20%. And according to the Zillow Group Consumer Housing Trends Report for 2018, younger sellers are more likely to navigate For Sale By Owner. Thirty-six percent of Millennials and twenty-six percent of Gen-Xers try to sell on their own. And in urban areas, where populations are younger, thirty-four percent of sellers are likely to try For Sale By Owner.

CAN A REALTOR GET MORE FOR YOUR HOME?

The National Association of Realtors claims that people who do For Sale By Owner *sell their homes for less*. But that is not true. They say that because they are comparing the average price for homes sold by the owners to the average price for homes sold by realtors. Initially, that might seem fair, until you consider this: the homes sold by owners are typically on the lower end of the market. People with lower-priced homes, who have lower income, can't afford realtor's fees, so they do For Sale By Owner. The lower price points of For Sale By Owner homes bring the average sold prices down. Comparing the average sale price of FSBO homes with that of realtor-sold homes doesn't mean realtors get more money when they sell homes. *It simply means they sell more expensive homes.*

But we can get an unbiased view by looking at a study of homes in Madison, Wisconsin, that adjusted for the price differences between homes typically sold by owners and homes sold by realtors found that *the actual difference in price between homes sold by owners and homes sold by realtors is 0%!* And not only is it not true that a realtor will get you a higher price, remember that any higher price will have to *more than cover the realtor's commission for it to be worth it.* So unless you are confident that a realtor can get you an offer that is over 5% higher (the typical commission) than you will get on your own, it's *not* financially advantageous to sell through a realtor.

And, if you are in a hurry to sell, you might take the typical 5% commission as a discount off the price of your home as an incentive for buyers, instead of paying a realtor. Not paying a realtor can allow you to put your house on the market at a discount, if a speedy sale is critical to you.

WHAT YOU SHOULD KNOW IF YOU CAN'T DO FSBO

When you list a home, especially in a market that has a scarcity of homes available, a realtor, trying to get your house listing, will often tell you that most For Sale By Owners fail. I retaliate with my previous success as a FSBO. Since my success negates that argument, they might then try to convince me that they would get more for my home than I will on my own. And the Wisconsin study shows *that* isn't true. In addition, they'd have to get a lot more for my home to cover their commission because if they can't, it's still not worth it to me. Even with my early training and success at doing For Sale By Owner, I still find it hard to resist the pressure of a friendly realtor offering to help me sell.

You might wonder why it matters to realtors if you sell your home or not, but in a good market, inventory of homes might be low, and the more homes a realtor is listing, the better the chances they have of making money. Also, it's in the realtor's best interest to discourage owners from selling on their own to protect their commissions and the industry the way it's structured. If everyone started selling their homes successfully and didn't need to pay thousands in realtors commissions, their industry would shrink.

Another argument a realtor might use to discourage you from selling on your own is that they have expertise in real estate and you don't. It's true that real estate comes with a lot of vocabulary, and since we usually only buy and sell homes a few times, it's not like we're practiced and expert at it.

One realtor told me she wouldn't dream of walking into my classroom (since I'm a teacher) without the years of training and experience I bring to the table, and conversely, I shouldn't consider myself an expert at real estate. I shouldn't be dabbling in something best left to the professionals, or I risk leaving money on the table.

In fact, I feel that teaching is an organic process that requires good communication skills and a desire to help someone, and absolutely believe lots of lay-people can be superb teachers. Similar to real estate, there are tasks that comprise both jobs that are simply hard work.

In my case I responded that I'd taken a course in real estate in college (so technical I'm as trained as they are), that my track record of selling three homes FSBO speaks for itself and, lastly, that I *always hire a knowledgeable real estate lawyer to represent me in all sales and to double-check the paperwork*, ensure than I am legally compliant, and to make sure I'm not missing anything. And real estate lawyers have a lot more training than a real estate agent, and are fully knowledgable about contracts and laws, so I don't have to be.

Be careful and have strong boundaries. Some realtors are high pressure, but it's served with a smile, so it's hard to tell when they are pushing you beyond what you are comfortable with. If you are unsure, or feel you are being pressured, always ask for 24 hours to think about it. Or a week. *Sign nothing* until you are certain, as a contract with a realtor is legally binding and may even exclude your right to sell the house on your own for the duration of the contract (or if you find a seller, the agent is still entitled to their commission). Read the contract carefully. Asking for a bit of time to think it over is perfectly reasonable, and if a realtor tries to pressure you to sign immediately, think about this: do you really want to work with a person who has their own needs ahead of yours?

You will be paying a realtor a sizable sum of money. Get your money's worth and get someone you'll be comfortable working with. There are some delightful, honest, and kind realtors out there, ones who enjoy helping people find a home or sell. Ask around for recommendations and ask why they are being recommended. "She's my friend" isn't a good reason. "She sold my home" is. Carefully consider if you want to hire a friend. This is a business transaction, one for which you will pay an *enormous* amount of money, perhaps the largest fee you will pay to any professional over the course of your life. Approach picking a realtor the same way you would pick a doctor, a lawyer, or any other person you need professional help from. If you pick a friend who's a realtor, how will they feel when the contract is up and you hire a different realtor? Which you should do, keeping the contract length as short as possible. Will you feel comfortable telling your realtor you think they need to do more to market your home? Your friendship may not survive. This is a big, costly decision. Make it carefully. Ask for sales numbers.

Hire the best realtor you can find. They all charge about the same, so why not?

I'd like to add an update here. In response to the new real estate commissions ruling that went into effect in August of 2024 (last months as I'm writing this), I'm seeing realtors list houses that say things like "Absolutely no showings unless you are represented by a qualified realtor!" And, there was a recent thread on Reddit where a qualified, cash buyer could not get the seller's agent to give them a showing. What this says to me is that the realtors are worried about their paychecks and are trying to keep the current system in place. But as a seller, watch out for your own interests, not those of the realtor or the real estate industry.

As a seller, you are going to be asked to sign paperwork that says you will pay the buyer's realtor, perpetuating the system that's always existed in most areas of the country. Your realtor will probably say that realtors won't favor your home if they know you won't pay them. Problem with this argument is that they can't hide your home from buyers, everything is online. You can refuse to pay the buyer's realtor, that's what the new law insures. And, the new rules state that it *won't be listed in your ad* whether or not you will pay the buyer's agent.

So agents can't avoid your home because they won't get paid, or will be paid a lower percentage than the standard. That's why realtors who are working with buyers are now being very careful to get a contract up front that says is the seller won't be paying them, at closing, then the buyer will have to.

You can offer to pay both realtors the way it's always worked, and I expect most sellers who list with a realtor will allow this perpetuation of the standard way of doing business. But I hope you won't let a buyer who approaches without a realtor, get turned away by your realtor saying, "no showings without a realtor!" Because they will be refusing a buyer that could have saved you half of the real estate commissions! My advice is to not to sign something requiring that you pay both commissions, but rather, that you will consider paying both if the offer works for you to do so. Perhaps you'll get an offer so high that asks for you to compensate the buyer's realtor, and another that doesn't, but the offer requiring agent's fees is significantly higher. And also, make sure your contract doesn't exclude buyers without realtors from seeing your home with your listing realtor! You can require pre qualification for a mortgage, and that might be an argument your listing agent will make, that you don't want an unrepresented and unqualified person wasting everyone's time. But a buyer can be unrepresented, and well-qualified, and the new real estate commissions laws may be bringing a lot more unrepresented buyers to the market because paying the realtor from the buyer's funds is brand new.

And, retain the ability to sell on your own if you find a buyer without a realtor. I recommend this because what if your brother-in-law's sister decides she wants to buy your home? The realtor shouldn't be paid unless their efforts found the buyer.

Should a qualified buyer contact you and say they can't get an appointment with your realtor, you not only have reason to fire your realtor, but it will be perfectly legal for you to be a FSBO and sell to that buyer. Read contracts carefully. Keep your rights, know what you're signing, consider having a real estate lawyer check out the contract if you have any confusion.

KNOW EXACTLY WHAT SERVICES YOUR REALTOR IS GOING TO PROVIDE (OR NOT)

When realtors came to my house to present their market analysis, they found me under stress as I worked to get my house and downtrodden yard ready for sale. And they offered to help! They would be my partner in this, they would do everything they could to help get the house ready for sale, they knew how hard this must be for me.

The empathy felt good. Tired and vulnerable, I almost bought it. But when I pressed for details, what they were really offering was this: they had the phone numbers of landscapers I could call. They had the numbers of people who stage homes for me to call (staging a home is something that a decorator can help you with; they come in and tell you how to make it look appealing to buyers). They would also give me the number for the junk removal service. But really, I would have to make all the calls and schedule the appointments with the landscapers — as I had been struggling to do already. There was no guarantee their landscaper would be any more available or affordable. I would pay lots of other people to do the work I'd been doing, before we sold the home, while money was tight. I could have called in a big dumpster and paid to have everything brought to the landfill, which would've been easier and faster, but I was trying to recycle, so I continued with hauling my donations to the local charity thrift stores. The promise of "I'll help you get the house ready!" was really just "I have contacts and phone numbers for you to call and hire people to get the house ready!" I didn't have a lot of cash on hand, so the work fell to me, even if I hired a realtor.

Be cautious, if they offer help. Ask exactly what they mean and what services your realtor includes. Some keep a decorator on staff for staging, or are very good at it themselves, so that might save you a couple hundred dollars and they can make an amazing difference in making your house appealing to buyers. But maybe you have friends who are good at this and would enjoy doing it for free. Ask who enjoys decorating (that's what I did). When in doubt, make the house look spacious and empty, and get rid of any personal items and pictures, as they distract from the home. You want people to be looking at your house, not pictures of your children or your vacation. You want to give them the opportunity to envision themselves in the home, which is harder if you've left lots of evidence that it's your home. Make it as generic as possible. See Chapter 8 for more advice on this.

A realtor will either do the photos and video for you, or hire a photographer who works for their brokerage. Make sure your realtor does great photography because in this age of internet shopping, the pics are the first view of your house your buyer will see (and maybe the last, if they aren't any good). Check out examples of their other house listings to see if you like the photography work.

Staging and photos of your home shouldn't cost more than a few hundred dollars, so that's all you're saving if a realtor offers these services for free, compared to the thousands you will pay in commissions.

AVOID THE FLAT FEE BROKER AND THE MLS (IMPORTANT!)

If you are reading this, you have a newer copy of my book. I'm going to leave this original story below, as a cautionary tale in finding a flat flee listing service you can trust, and because it will help you to test out your flat fee listing broker and insure they are doing right by you.

But my advice has changed due to how Zillow, the most popular site for people looking for homes, treats for sale by owner homes.

In the past, a for sale by owner home listing, free on Zillow, was listed the same as all the other homes. And you could, in your ad copy, identify yourself as a for sale by owner who was happy to work with buyers, and direct them to your copy information.

Zillow, perhaps in response to realtor's objections, now has all for sale by owner properties in a separate tab, and buyers have to remember to click on that tab.

I've looked recently, and there are precious few for sale buy owner listings. But I think this is misleading, because what has happened is that more people are using the flat fee listing, just like I did when I sold this house. You can read below on why I didn't think it was the correct way to go, and what went wrong for me.

But because it's become more common, I thing there are companies willing to do flat fee who will pass on your contact information to buyers without an issue.

So, I highly recommend now that you do use a flat fee listing to get your home before buyers in the same tab as all the other homes. And, one of the nice things about the new real estate commissions rules of 2024 is that the percentage you pay (if any) to real estate agents who bring you a buyer will no longer be listed in the MLS. So agents can't avoid your house or talk your buyer out of seeing the house because you are paying a reduced commission. Or because you aren't paying any commission to realtors. They can call you up and negotiate ahead of bringing their buyers, and perhaps you can say you will pay them a fee, or you can tell them you won't decide until you see the entire offer, or that you won't no matter what, in which case the agent would go back to their buyers and say they won't represent them in this purchase or bring them to see the house. It's all up to you.

I wonder if there will be any good statistics about selling for sale by owner, because anything listed with the flat fee broker is going to be identified as sold by a realtor, even if it was a for sale by owner.

If you want more information about flat fee listings, the FSBO subreddit (on Reddit, a collection of communities where people discuss topics of interest) has lots of postings and advice about picking a flat fee listing broker.

Below you'll also see that I ended up having to pay a buyer's realtor, though at a discount, because the people who bought my house had a buyer's realtor. If you are listed as a flat fee listing, there *isn't a way for a buyer to know* you are for sale buy owner, so assume that you are paying both realtors, and bring their own, because in the past (before the new real estate commission law of August 2024) it was free to them. In reality, both buyer and seller could have saved paying any commission (and perhaps the buyer get the house for less) if the buyer had just contacted the seller directly. And today, because the buyer may be required to pay their own realtor, they might appreciate the ability to purchase without a realtor on either side. In any case, a buyer would do well to always call a listing realtor and find out if the home is indeed a for sale buy owner. They might still want to have a realtor on their side, but they should check and see if the seller will be paying for that. I offered a reduced commission, and negotiated it down further once the offer was made, because that realtor did barely any work.

That concludes my update in response to the way Zillow lists For Sale By Owners. As you continue to read, you'll learn more about the flat fee listing process, including the unfortunate way it played out for me.

If you hire a realtor, they will enter your ad into the Multiple Listing Service, otherwise known as MLS. Realtors created the Multiple Listing Service for realtors so they can see each other's listings. Otherwise, you would have to go to one brokerage to see their homes, and another to see the listing of a different brokerage. Entering your home into the MLS distributes it to all real estate searching web sites.

If you don't hire a realtor, you can still get your home into the MLS. A search for "flat fee broker" will turn up realtors who will list you in MLS for just that, a flat fee. This means that a realtor, for a onetime set price (a flat fee — usually \$100-\$200 — and not a commission based on a percentage of the sale price of your house) will allow you to enter your house's ad in the MLS. They restrict access to entering listings into the MLS to realtors. In the previous chapter I mentioned that I did a flat-fee MLS listing for my last home sale, and when buyers saw my ad the listing identified me as "For Sale By Owner" and had my contact information. That's changed, which is a problem, but there's nothing you can do about it. Realtors tightly control the MLS. As it was explained to me, it was created by realtors, for realtors, and there isn't a decent alternative. Yet.

At first, I thought I was lucky that some realtors will allow a For Sale By Owner ad into the MLS at a reasonable cost. I figured that the flat-fee listing realtor is hoping that if you don't sell, they will get your home listing when you give up. I paid \$99 for my listing. Though I sold my last house with MLS, *I no longer advise anyone to use a flat-fee MLS listing service.* At first I thought I was lucky, but now I view this as the biggest mistake I made with my most recent sale.

I needed to list my home online, and I thought putting the home into MLS was the best way to do so. It would be in the MLS, obviously, but the MLS also feeds the other sites, like Zillow.com. But here's what I learned: when you list this way, they put your home into MLS *under the flat fee broker who took your listing*. Then, when it goes into the real estate sites that people use to search for homes, there are other realtors listed on the page who have paid for advertising on that site. My flat fee broker was there, too, but she wasn't even the first in the list! Maybe the arrangement on the list reflects what realtors have paid for that advertising space. This is a problem, because that flat fee broker is the one I need to pass on my contact information to anyone who calls, *and* to inform them I am doing For Sale By Owner. There was no way for a buyer to tell who the original flat-fee listing realtor is. Mine didn't even show up on the real estate page when I went to check my listing out. The realtors listed on my page were whoever had paid to be there. They had no connection to me or my home. If I was a buyer, I would call the top realtor on that list, assuming they were the listing agent. They put a buyer calling on my home in touch with a realtor who has paid to advertise there. This entitles the agent to the commission I offered to pay to realtors who bring me a buyer. I expected to pay realtors who brought me a buyer, but in this case, I was providing the ad through my flat-fee listing. Instead of it helping to bring me buyers directly, I had realtors advertising on my page, confusing buyers and practically guaranteeing that I'd have to pay a realtor a commission.

I like to tell you about two important experiences I had,

hoping you will learn from them and not make the same mistake I did in listing my property.

I occasionally would get a call from a realtor who'd called the flat-fee broker, and the broker had given the realtor my number because they had a buyer that wanted to see my home. I never once had a buyer get the number from the flat-fee broker and call me without being represented by a realtor. My guess is that people who are buying a house often work with their own realtor and sometimes sign a contract with that agent as a buyer-broker. The seller still pays the agent, but buyers see all the homes with "their" agent. So if they want to see a house, my house, they called their agent and ask them to arrange it. Looking at my ad online, *there was absolutely no way for them to know that I was For Sale By Owner* and that they might save some money by contacting me directly, because the MLS doesn't allow you to specify in your ad you are For Sale By Owner. For this reason, I wish I'd never listed in the MLS. Instead, if I had listed directly in other real estate websites, like Zillow.com, my ad would have identified my home as a For Sale By Owner and my contact information would have gone right in the ad. There's no flat-fee-listing real estate agent as a middleman.

I got very few calls from realtors with my MLS ad. I was curious why I wasn't getting calls, so I had a friend call up my flat fee broker, the one who had placed my home in MLS. She pretended she was a buyer interested in my home. A man answered, a realtor who worked in my listing agent's office. He said he would be happy to show her the house. Surprised he didn't give her my contact information and instead offered to act as her realtor, she persisted, asking, "Isn't that home For Sale By Owner?"

At first he said, "Oh, I don't think so, let me look." When he came back to the call he said it was, and told my friend, "You probably don't want to get involved in that, owners are notoriously hard to deal with." She continued to press him for the contact information and he finally gave her my number.

I was livid. Based on that interaction, I could probably sue my realtor for false advertising. I expected anyone at her agency to put interested buyers in touch with me. Instead, someone in her office was obstructing an interested buyer's access to my contact information, trying to get her to use him as a realtor and requiring me to pay him a fee. If you use a flat-fee broker and list in MLS anyway, make sure you have someone call up and test this for you to ensure that they inform people that you are For Sale By Owner and that they freely give your contact information out. But because of my experience, *I would not recommend listing this way*. It's almost guaranteed you will pay at least one realtor's commission if you do.

The second part of my caution against using flat fee listings in the MLS is when I tested this as a buyer.

Once my house sold, I rented an apartment but I also started looking for a new home to purchase. I saw an open house in a town I liked on a Sunday afternoon. I went to several homes in that town on a Sunday, and when I drove up to one it had an enormous banner out front, that said "For Sale By Owner!"

I met the owner, a young man who'd renovated the home himself. I told him the home was too small for me, but I wished him luck in the process and said I'd just sold my fourth home For Sale By Owner. We high-fived each other.

He said he'd also paid a flat fee for an MLS listing, which is why it wasn't clear to me it was For Sale By Owner until I arrived and saw his banner. This is a problem, because if I have a realtor, if I believe a home is listed with a realtor, I'll bring mine so they can represent me. The seller has to pay 5% whether it's all for their listing realtor, who represents them, or if they have to split it with a buyer's agent who represents *me*. Why wouldn't I bring a realtor in on my side, as long as I believe the house is already being sold by a real estate agent? You can buy without a realtor, and I describe how and why you might want to do so in Chapter 6. If, however, you prefer working with your realtor and you know the buyer is paying the commission, unless there are a lot of buyers competing for the home, there's isn't any reason you shouldn't bring yours. But if I don't bring a realtor because I know the property is For Sale By Owner, that owner has lots more wiggle room in negotiating a price with me, possibly saving *me* money on the purchase.

When I did For Sale By Owner, I preferred to sell to a buyer directly so I would save having to pay any commissions. Having a house in MLS would be fine if it increased traffic or brought buyers who will only work with realtors, but as I mentioned, I discovered the hard way that it didn't work that way. No realtor brought me buyers, even the ones who said they had people lined up to buy when they were trying to get my listing.

This owner said he was certain that his flat-fee realtor was giving out his contact information. So I said, "Let's check that out." I looked up his ad and called the number for his flat-fee-listing ad. I left a message on the realtor's voicemail that I was interested in the home at his address. It took well over 48 hours for the realtor to return my call. After 24 hours, I emailed the owner telling him I hadn't heard from his realtor. When she called, she left a message apologizing for the delay, but didn't inform me that his house was For Sale By Owner, or leave his contact information! Instead, she said, "There's the property you called on, and there's another in the same neighborhood. Would you like to go see them? I'd be happy to show them to you." Essentially, she was asking to be my buyer-broker. This isn't what I expected the buyer's experience would be when inquiring about a home listed with a flat-fee listing in MLS. I thought I'd be told that the home was a For Sale By Owner and get the owner's contact information. Even now, I occasionally get a text from her asking if I'd like to see homes in that town, with no mention of the fact that I had originally called on a For Sale By Owner home. I never got his contact information from her. When I wrote to him a few weeks later and told him what her message said, he said that he had a contract with her that said if she brought a buyer to him, she would get a co-broke fee. But I had approached him on my own first. And her becoming my realtor isn't the point of a flat-fee listing. Or, at least, it isn't for those of us selling homes on our own, or for those of us who are happy to buy directly from owners. With his MLS listing buyers still couldn't reach him directly. The flat-fee realtor inserted herself into the middle of the deal.

For these reasons — the way they list the ads in MLS and the way they handle calls — you are likely to have to pay a co-broke fee if you use the MLS. No one knows you are For Sale By Owner, and even calling the flat-fee listing broker can make it difficult for a buyer to get in touch with a For Sale By Owner.

In Chapter 8 I'll give advice on how to handle this differently, and what I told friends who sold after me. But I listed with MLS, and I'll continue to describe how I did that. This information applies whether or not you use MLS, as you will still want to be online with some service. Do some research about what is the best route when it comes time for you to sell, but right now Zillow.com seems to lead the pack, and you can easily identify as a For Sale By Owner when you list on their site.

PREPARING INFORMATION TO LIST ONLINE

Everyone looks for homes online these days, so you must list online no matter which site you go with. To prepare to list online, gather your facts about your house. Collect room sizes, special features, style of house, floor plans, pictures as digital images (jpegs) you or your photographer took of your home, and sit down to fill out the information online. Today the sites will use your address to pull information from the registry of deeds for tax information and such, which is nice. I had my floor plans for the house from when we built it, so I had the room sizes all set to go as they were on the building plans. I also took pictures of the floor plans and included them in the collection of pictures. If you have a realtor, they'll measure the rooms for you. You may have to measure yours if you don't have a floor plan. People want to know if their bedroom furniture will fit. It probably took me an hour or two to get it done and upload the pictures. This is time-consuming and detail-oriented, not great fun for ADD types, but you only have to do it once. You can update after if you need to, but that's easier and then you'll know the system. The sites also walk you through it, so it's not difficult, just tedious. If you have all the info about your house at the ready, you can probably get it all done in about an hour. Make sure you write down the room sizes and other information (like your house description) before you start in on filling out the form online. That way, if something goes wrong and you lose the data as you're entering it, you'll at least have it written down and can start over. I had a folder on my computer that had all the pictures and a file with the description of the house. This I changed nearly weekly once I listed to fine-tune it to market the property better, as the house description is a very important part of your ad. Later I'll coach you on writing that well.

A realtor will be good at entering the ad into the online system, as they do it all the time, but it's not anything out of reach of your abilities. A detailed form will guide you to enter details about your house with specifics like: room sizes, number of bedrooms, number and type of bathrooms (1/2, 3/4, or full), type of heating or cooling system, appliances included, garage size, and amenities, that kind of thing. You'll check off on lots of toggle items like whether your property is waterfront or has a view, that kind of thing.

OFFERING A CO-BROKE FEE TO REALTORS

When you enter your ad online is when you decide if and how much you'll offer as a co-broke fee to realtors. Why pay a realtor if you're selling the house yourself? Because most buyers pick a realtor to work with when they are searching for a home. Though in the past it was the seller paying both realtors, the buyer's agent is working as a "buyer broker," meaning they are representing the interests of the buyer, taking them to see homes, sending them emails of homes listings that might interest them. Some people will pay out of pocket as a buyer to hire a broker who will work for them as buyer-broker, but this is unusual. The seller pays the agent for bringing the buyer to them when the house sells. So you need to ask yourself if you will pay realtors who bring a buyer to you, or those realtors brought in by buyers because they are more comfortable working with them.

Updating this for the new real estate commissions rules, this is even more important to consider now. You are no longer expected to pay a buyer's realtor, and because the rule changed has had so much press, lots of buyers are wary to enter into a contract that might require them to pay the commission of their own realtor. You can always offer a commission, with the hope that more realtors will bring customers to you, or maybe you will reach customers who are only comfortable working with a buyer's realtor.

I included a normal co-broke fee of 2.5% for my area when I listed my home in MLS. I may have been naive in thinking brokers will work with me as a For Sale By Owner because they would make the same as they would in any sale (the normal commission for real estate here is 5%, with 2.5% going to each broker, listing and buyer). Realtors want to avoid helping For Sale By Owners, and I wish I'd just put in 0.5% commission, or maybe 1%. It may have eliminated buyer brokers from helping me at all, but the *only* realtors that came were those the buyers brought after they came to see the home at an open house, or buyers who saw my home online and not knowing it was For Sale By Owner, asked their broker to contact me. Unfortunately for the buyer, when this happened it meant I had about $18,000 less negotiating dollars to deal with. I'd rather cut the price on my home for the buyer than pay a realtor. So decide when you get to this point where you stand, and how much of an incentive you want to offer realtors to bring you buyers.

I think it's telling that the two realtors who were trying to get my listing and gave me their market analysis, who assured me they had buyers just waiting for a house like mine, or claimed they had access to hundreds of buyers, didn't bother to bring *even one* to see the house once I listed as For Sale By Owner, despite the offer of the same commission rate they would make on any other house. Either they didn't really want to help me, or they didn't really have those buyers lined up and just wanted my listing.

I don't mean to disparage all realtors; I understand they are trying to make a living and protect the way they do so. But I also feel like I should have the right to sell my home on my own. I understand that making that decision means I'm unlikely to get any help selling, even if I offer a great commission.

When I got impatient, I even tried listing it for a couple weeks at 3% — a higher co-broke fee than a realtor would normally get — and even that didn't change a thing. Draw your own conclusion, but mine is that realtors will not help you unless a buyer asks them to see your house. They're just keeping the lines of communication open for when you give up, when they hope to get you as a client. But as long as you are advertising where buyers will see it, online, a realtor's help isn't necessary.

My friends who did For Sale By Owner offered a commission of 1% to any agent who brought a buyer. I think this is reasonable, given the price of local homes, for a broker who will do little more than attend a showing, an inspection, and a closing. In my case, that would have been about $6,000. My lawyer would even take care of drawing up contracts and closing details, so that would mean minimal work for the realtor.

If you get a realtor who brings you a buyer and wants more that 1%, they can negotiate that as part of the offer. Perhaps the offer will be so good, you'll be willing to pay the realtor more, which happened to another friend who did FSBO recently. The buyers offered above asking, so it was a straightforward decision to pay the realtor an additional 1%.

The bottom line is that realtors can't hide your home if you list it online. If a buyer sees it and wants to go look, the realtor can bow out if they don't want to work for a reduced commission. If I was a buyer, I would want to see every house that appealed to me, and I'd go directly to the seller, or attend an open house, and find out how I could buy that house on my own.

THE MOST IMPORTANT MARKETING AFTER PICTURES: YOUR HOUSE DESCRIPTION

To list online you will need to write up a description of your home, and I prepared to do this for my MLS listing. I had a limited amount of space; I believe it was around 2500 characters, so I needed to choose words carefully to capture the buyer's interest. To get started, look online at similar homes and gather phrases you like. Do not violate fair-housing rules by mentioning national origin, race, gender, disability or familial status! My flat-flee broker even made me take out the phrase "family room" because it implied I would only sell to families. I also had to remove "teen hangout/movie room." I didn't care who bought my house, I had only wanted to convey that I'd designed the house for a large family with kids (mine) and another family might enjoy the features I'd included to make living in the house with kids easier. But fair housing laws require that you avoid mentioning people or types of people. So I had to take out the phrase "family." But families know what they are looking for anyway, and the large mud room will appeal to them all on its own, or maybe it will appeal to someone who's single but has lots of dogs. Who knows? Anyway, don't limit who you will sell to because it's illegal! And you want to throw your net as wide as possible.

Here are the iterations of my house description. I probably changed it weekly. I was trying to entice buyers to come to see the home.

Here is my first try:

"Remarkable, Spacious Cape Designed for Easy Living! Expansive Kitchen open to Gathering Room overlooking large back yard, a treed hill, multi-level decks, and above-ground pool with wrap-around deck. Walk-in Pantry has natural light and custom-built open shelving. Master bedroom's bathroom en suite has a claw-foot tub and a walk-in closet. Two bedrooms open onto a playroom/hangout/music room roughed for a home theater. Got stuff? Entry hall from the garage has a cleaning closet, mudroom, and bonus room for laundry, office, or gear room! Basement is roughed for finishing. The 2x6 home has oversized windows, hardwood, tile. High ceiling in the 3-car garage. The generous custom molding includes 8 inch baseboards and horizontal 5-panel doors. 9-foot ceilings on 1st floor. Quiet rural town has terrific schools and abundant conservation land and trails. Walk to lake beach. All only 10 minutes from restaurants and shops!"

I was looking to sell quickly so I could move on with my life and settle the last of the divorce. I was very impatient, and it was the middle of the summer. People shopping for houses were fewer as many were on vacation. But, I panicked and dropped the price $20,000 to $628,000, and added these two sentences to the beginning of the ad:

"Drastic price reduction! Motivated Sellers!"

Never do that. It sounds desperate, and I think people wonder what's wrong with your house you had to drop the price by so much. Dropping the price causes a notice to go out to anyone who saved or liked your house anyway, so no other commentary is necessary.

I tried a new write up to generate more interest and tried harder to focus on how great this house is for family living:

> "Unique and Expansive Cape built for Family Living! Open concept Kitchen and Family Room overlook multi-level decks, fields, and woods, above ground pool with wrap-around deck. Walk-in Pantry has natural light and custom-built open shelving. Master bedroom's spacious bathroom en suite includes a claw-foot tub and a walk-in closet. Two bedrooms open onto a play-room/teen hangout/music room roughed for a home theater. Entry hall from the garage has a cleaning closet, mudroom, and bonus room for laundry, office, or gear room. Basement is roughed for finishing, prepped for a bathroom, HVAC installed, includes a sliding glass door and lots of full-sized windows. The 2x6 Modular constructed home has over-sized windows, hard-wood and tile. 3-car garage has high ceilings. 2nd floor laundry. The generous custom molding includes 8 inch baseboards and lovely horizontal 5-panel doors. 9 foot ceilings on 1st floor.
>
> A beautiful space for everyone and everything!
>
> Call 555-555-5555."

I listed my number right in the description this time because I suspected that my flat-fee realtor wasn't passing on leads or inquiries from buyers. And, I'd noticed that when my listing appeared in other sites like (Zillow or Trulia), there were lots of realtors pictured for people to contact, but no direct way for them to see or contact me.

But in MLS you can't put your number in the ad. I was told by my listing-only broker that the MLS is for realtors only, and therefore, the phone calls had to go through her office, and she would forward the buyers to me. This did not happen, not even once. If I put in an open house, people came, and then I could tell them I was For Sale By Owner, but most people work with realtors today and they bring their realtor into the middle of the negotiations, anyway. She also told me to take out the word "family," as it violated fair housing laws.

CAREFULLY CRAFT YOUR HOUSE DESCRIPTION

That's when I finally looked at this as a writing problem and it needed a writing solution. I was marketing my house to a home buyer. I wanted the buyer to fall in love with my house, and to see themselves living there. Saying it had a large garage and a walk-in closet would not fire up the imagination of the buyer. Besides, the measurements and description elsewhere in the ad gave a factual accounting of what the house contained. I didn't have to say it was large, that was clear by the square footage listed below the description. I also didn't need to report that there was a claw-foot tub, as it was pictured in the bathroom photo.

DOING RESEARCH ON WRITING HOUSE DESCRIPTIONS

I started my research by looking at the real estate ads in the more expensive homes of surrounding wealthier towns. I figured that the best realtors would want to be selling the more expensive homes where they stand to make the biggest commission on sales. I learned a lot from looking at these ads. Here's a sample:

"New home with finishing touches in progress! One of the most SOUGHT AFTER LOCATIONS IN ALL OF WEALTHYFORD combined with a LUXURIOUS ABSOLUTELY DESIGN

SENSITIVE INTERIOR make this HOME the best purchase in this price range!!! Custom finishes and a perfect scale contribute to this property's TIMELESS AESTHETIC. Designed by A NOTEWORTHY LOCAL ARCHITECT.... the floor plan is spectacular with too many CUSTOM DETAILS TO LIST!! Walkability, indoor and outdoor entertaining spaces, an ample yard, custom finishes, FOUR floors of finished space all with BUILT INS/CUSTOM MILLWORK throughout. This 5 bedroom 4.5 bathroom home is on par with those properties featured in today's design magazines!! Third floor space with private bath makes for the perfect au pair/teen/guest space. The neighborhood is active and inviting and is just a short walk to the QUAINT downtown!"

What I noticed is that the ads had lots of *feeling words and phrases*. They hinted at the experience of living in the home advertised instead of just listing features.

I read a lot of them and made a list of the emotion-evoking words and phrases they contained that could apply to my house. See if you agree that they are amazing:

- Remarkable
- Thoughtfully constructed
- Sip coffee on decks or dine alfresco
- Gleaming hardwood
- Superb
- Grand rooms
- Upscale
- Dramatic
- Backdrop of panoramic views
- Desirable neighborhood
- Spectacular

- Too many custom details to list
- Ample yard
- Inviting neighborhood
- Luxurious
- Absolutely design-sensitive interior
- Fabulous family home
- Brilliantly
- Short distance from
- Convenience
- Comfortable
- Entertainment sized
- Daylight basement (sounds better than "walk-out")
- Masterfully crafted
- Relaxing lifestyle
- Extended family
- Best purchase in this price range
- Great value
- Perfect scale and timeless aesthetic
- Sought-after location

I determined that rather than say the master bath had a claw-foot tub, I needed to convey how much the new owner would enjoy relaxing in a claw-foot tub of their own. Describe the *feeling* the special features of this home would elicit, rather than a factual listing of what the home contains.

I also noticed the expensive homes' ads had LOTS of CAPITALIZATION.

Now that I knew I needed to sell an emotion and experience, and armed with my new vocabulary, I attempted to get my buyer to fall in love with my home by having them fall in love with how their life will feel when they live there. I re-wrote the ad, making generous use of my shift key, and came up with the following:

> "REMARKABLE SPACIOUS CAPE DESIGNED FOR EASY LIVING AND ENTERTAINING! Sip coffee or dine alfresco on the SPACIOUS TIERED DECKS overlooking ample backyard and dramatic treed hillside backdrop. Invite friends to enjoy the pool and relax on the WRAP AROUND DECK. DESIRABLE INVITING RURAL NEIGHBORHOOD a short, convenient drive to SHOPPING AND DINING. WALK TO LAKE BEACH and conservation trails. SPECTACULAR MASTER BEDROOM SUITE provides a relaxing SANCTUARY WITH CLAW-FOOT SOAKING TUB and an enormous walk-in closet. BRILLIANTLY DESIGNED INTERIOR has space for everyone and everything, pantry with custom shelving, mud room, large laundry, abundant NATURAL LIGHT. Invite guests or extended family and entertain downstairs and up, as an ENTERTAINMENT-SIZED PLAYROOM/HOBBY ROOM gives guests lots of space to spread out and has hooks for home theater. DAYLIGHT BASEMENT is rough finished for more entertainment space. 2x6 constructed, oversized insulated garage, masterfully crafted FABULOUS HOME!"

I enjoy writing and usually write fiction. But writing this new ad appealed to the creative writer in me as I tried to paint a comforting picture of the new owner's future living in my home, pulling from my personal experience of what *I* enjoyed about my home and the neighborhood. I wanted them to imagine themselves drinking coffee outside in nature, walking to the lake, enjoying movies in a home theater, the spa-like experience of soaking in an oversized tub. They would do a lot of entertaining! I found it interesting that this was an exercise in creative (though truthful) writing, and I believe yours should be, too. They can see the room measurements in the listing and they can see that you have a three-car garage, so there's no need to repeat those facts again in your description. What you need in the description is a *vision.* You want to evoke for the buyer the vision of how wonderful it will be to live in your house. Describe what you have loved about living in your home.

Don't be afraid to brag about your home. Phrases like "Great friendly neighborhood!" or "Walking distance to conservation trails" or "Convenient to shopping" already evoke imaginings of the life they will have if they buy your house. What's been your favorite part of living there, and what makes your home stand out? Make sure you include those, with as many feeling words as possible. Here's a list of feeling words I compiled that might help you get in the mood to describe your home. See if you can write a description to invoke the picture they paint, or sprinkle them into your own house description:

FEELING WORDS TO USE IN DESCRIBING YOUR HOME

- Home
- Sanctuary
- Dwelling
- Snug, cozy (though these will imply "small")
- Luxury
- Safety
- Sentiment: pride, ownership

- Friendly
- Comfortable
- Company
- Friends
- Nature
- Bright
- Sunny
- Private
- Quiet
- Convenience
- Spacious
- Ease

NEWLY WRITTEN AD SELLS THE HOME

Writing the description this new way worked! Many more people attended the next few open houses. I hosted two per weekend now, my ex-husband took the first Saturday after re-writing this ad, and I took the Sunday. He had a constant stream of buyers looking at the house, and they spent lots of time. Two of the couples who came on Saturday came back on Sunday. I would also advise you to try back-to-back open houses. It gives people two low-key, low-pressure ways to check the house out at their leisure. Open houses that realtors run are usually earlier in the day, if you can make your open house longer or hold your open house later in the day, you might increase traffic. Some buyers spend the entire day driving to open houses, so adding your open house after the others are over will be a no-brainer, scheduling-wise. And the open houses are one of the best ways, as a For Sale By Owner, to market your home. Just allow an interested buyer to fall in love with it and imagine themselves living there. The rest will be easy.

By the Tuesday after the weekend the new house description went live we received a full-price offer!

OFFER FALLS THROUGH DUE TO HOME INSPECTION SURPRISES

But an offer is not a closed sale, so be careful of getting too excited before closing. It's not over until it's over. This full-price offer fell through.

The couple who made the full price offer had come back for the second open-house day with the realtor they were working with. We had to pay this realtor 2.5% since I had listed that as our co-broke fee even though the realtor hadn't brought them to us, they'd just come after seeing our open house online. Regardless, we were happy. It was, after all, a full-price offer.

We scheduled an inspection within a week. The realtor said she had an inspector already lined up. We were confident that our 10-year-young house wouldn't have any difficulty passing inspection. But the inspector came and told the buyers that the roof needed replacing, that there were no cement footings under our deck supports, that the furnace might fail if we hadn't been properly maintaining it, that the marriage wall that bowed out slightly between the two modular boxes in the staircase was a sign of a "big problem," and several other scary things about our home. The roof was a total surprise to us, as the shingles were 20-year shingles and the house was only about 10 years old.

The other things he said were lies or conjecture, and we pointed out that the marriage wall bump was there from the beginning and wasn't a sign of a problem. Rather, getting a modular house to line up when the crane dropped the boxes in place is difficult (the bump was barely noticeable). And there were cement footings under the deck posts; if the inspector had moved some crushed stone at the base of the posts, he would have seen them. Our furnace had been under a maintenance contract for as long as we'd had the house. There was no need for the inspector to issue that dire warning. I said we'd look into the roof, but since all the other things the inspector pointed out weren't problems, we didn't believe the roof needed replacing soon either. The realtor didn't want to hear any of it. She told us her clients were disappointed and were pulling out of the sale. There was nothing we could do. It didn't matter that we felt the inspector had lied. Short of suing him (which we considered, the report felt that libelous), we would not get these buyers back, he had scared them off. We knew how solidly we constructed our home, so this news wasn't all that terrible. The only outstanding issue was the roof.

We called the real estate agent for a different buyer who'd made a low offer before the last open house, telling her we'd accept her client's offer if they came up by $10,000 and the realtor reduced her commission from the 2.5%, which was our co-broke fee, to 2%. The realtor immediately agreed to the 2%, and the buyers agreed to the increase. We didn't immediately inform them about a potential issue with the roof, as we weren't sure if it really was a problem, still thinking it might have been the inspector exaggerating. But we put in calls to roofers, and after a couple inspections and estimates we realized the shingles were failing prematurely. It wasn't failing or leaking yet, but shingles were curling and the company who had made them had horrible reviews. Our roof, though not ready to go at any minute, wouldn't make it another 10 years. We let the new buyers know and re-negotiated the price based on our estimates to fix it.

DISCLOSING INFORMATION ABOUT HOME PROBLEMS

To be clear, we went back to an original low-offer buyer because we were in a hurry. Once we knew the actual condition of the roof, we could repair it and put the house back on the market. Or, we could list it again disclosing the problem with the shingles, and it would affect the price anyway. Repairing and re-listing with a new roof was more time consuming, and also, the roof wasn't failing yet. It wouldn't need replacing for a few years.

If you know there is a problem with your home, you must disclose it. Ask your attorney how disclosures work and what you need to tell buyers about. For example, you might need to disclose the presence of lead paint. *Do not hide problems with your house!* Even though we hadn't known about the roof, once the buyers found out about the problem, they walked away from the sale. They believed we'd tried hiding information from them. No amount of assuring them we didn't, that the problem with the roof caught us off guard, or our offer to repair it, made them feel better. It was especially disappointing because the addition of the other things the inspector claimed were wrong with our house made the buyers even more skittish. I still wonder how that deal fell through, knowing the quality of my home. But a home purchase is a personal, sensitive thing, and you can't force anyone to be happy with your home, or logic them into it.

When our new buyers' inspector came, we pointed out the biggest problems the first inspector had, showed him the cement footings holding up the deck posts, and pointed out the bump in the staircase where the modular home boxes came together. This inspector lived in a modular home himself and assured our new buyers that it was perfectly normal and that this small flaw came with a lot of positives of having a modular constructed house.

HIRING A HOME INSPECTOR TO AVOID SURPRISES

Hiring your own house inspector can head off problems later when you get an offer. This costs some money, but if the report is good, you can offer it with other sales materials at the open houses. Had we done this, we might have found out about the roof, replaced it, and kept that full-price offer on the house.

That's the end of the story of the most recent sale. The negotiations with this buyer continued to be hard. Haggling over the ultimate price was difficult because their estimate of the roof repair was tens of thousands beyond our estimates. They even sent a person up on our roof without our permission.

We relied on our real estate attorney's communication throughout this process. And she was worth her weight in gold. We finally closed on the home, paying a realtor 2% of the price, and saving thousands more. In Chapter 8 I'll explain how I could have saved myself even more on this sale.

VIEW WITH CAUTION REALTOR'S ADVICE AGAINST FOR SALE BY OWNER

Because it's important, I'll summarize once again the arguments realtors make against doing For Sale By Owner — in an attempt to get a listing — along with rebuttals:

"Buyers at this price point won't want to deal with a For Sale By Owner."

Rebuttal: Buyers will do whatever they need to do to buy your home if they love it. If they see it online (and they can search anywhere in the country), there's every reason for them to come see it, and they won't be put off by a For Sale By Owner.

They might even guess — often correctly — that it could save them money, as the savings of paying a realtor don't have to land completely in the seller's pocket. Not having to pay a realtor's fee gives you more negotiating room, which might make the difference for the buyer and get the house sold.

"We can reach relocations as we are nationwide."

Rebuttal: As long as you list your home online, you have the reach you need to find buyers wherever they are searching from.

"We have the experience to get you the most money for your house. Realtors sell homes for more than For Sale By Owners."

Rebuttal: Realtors use the fact that people with lower-priced homes are more likely to do For Sale By Owner (as the savings in equity are more important to them than to wealthier clients) to imply that realtors get more money for houses *they* sell. But they get more money, on average, *because they sell more expensive homes than FSBO owners do.* A 2007 study of single-family homes sold in Madison, Wisconsin compared the prices of For Sale By Owner and realtor-assisted sales of similar homes in similar neighborhoods. The study found *no price difference at all* between comparable homes sold as For Sale By Owner and homes sold by realtors.

"I have a buyer looking for a home just like this in your town. They are eager to buy quickly."

Rebuttal: If a realtor says they have buyers lined up, offer them a reasonable co-broke fee to bring the buyers to you.

"The online estimates for your home value are not accurate. You need a real market analysis by a professional real estate agent to price your home correctly. Realtors have important knowledge that a layperson doesn't."

Rebuttal: The process is unfamiliar but much less complicated than most people think. Using this book guides you through being a For Sale By Owner, including pricing correctly. And hiring a real estate attorney can help guide you so you feel confident in signing contracts.

"You'll be wasting your time with people who can't afford your home. We will pre-qualify buyers for you."

Rebuttal: Most buyers self-select. They don't shop and look at homes that they can't afford because it's a waste of their time. And banks now offer pre-approval letters stating exactly what they can afford. You can request one when they submit an offer.

"Most For Sale By Owners fail."

Rebuttal: I've been successful every time I've sold For Sale By Owner and know others who have also had success. While writing this book, I've shared the information with four friends who sold without realtors, and one who bought without a realtor, and I also bought by myself without a realtor. Doing FSBO is getting easier and more widely accepted every day. According to the National Association of Realtors, in 2018 owners sold 11%

of homes in the US without a realtor. That number, though, doesn't include people who used a flat-fee listing in MLS (paying a minimal price to a realtor, say $99, to have your home put into the Multiple Listing Service but receiving no other help from the realtor) which accounts for an additional 10% of sales. The National Association of Realtors (NAR) counts flat-fee listings as realtor-assisted sales, *not* For Sale By Owner. I've sold four homes without realtors but only two of them would count as For Sale By Owner according to the NAR because on the two most recent I paid for a flat-fee listing in the MLS. So, upwards of 20% of homeowners are having success as For Sale By Owner.

CHAPTER 5 BOTTOM LINE

- Selling a house and moving is time-consuming, stressful and hard, with or without a realtor to help.
- **Pricing right is critical to selling quickly. Do your own research and price your house based on recent sales in your location.**
- If a realtor is asking to be your selling agent, make sure you know what services they include, what percentage you will pay, and how they will help you sell. Do they have someone to stage your home? Take pictures? What else will they do to market your home? Can you negotiate the commission? Will you be paying the buyer's realtor? Remember that you will most likely be paying tens of thousands of dollars to this person. If you hire someone, treat it with the seriousness and care it deserves. Hire a

professional, and do your research on hiring a great realtor.

- Be cautious of the hard sell from agents wanting to represent you, and don't sign a contract until you are comfortable. Take 24 hours to think it over. Consider a shorter term contract and keep the right to sell to buyers on your own.
- List in MLS with a flat-fee listing because then buyers will see your house, in the place where all the homes are listed and to in the separate for sale by owner tab in Zillow. You may decide to still pay a buyer-broker's commission. Call and test the flat fee realtor, make sure that they are sending prospective buyers directly to you, and not actively blocking access or trying to represent the buyer's who are calling on your house.
- Sellers who try For Sale By Owner can succeed. More (and younger) owners are selling this way, and it's *not true* that realtors will sell your home for more than you will yourself.
- If you are writing up your ad online, first write the information and description in a file on your computer, in case the website fails or quits before you finish. That way you have a saved copy and can recover or make changes easily.
- I've never had a realtor bring a buyer when I was For Sale By Owner, even though I listed with a co-broke for 2.5-3.0%. It was always a buyer who brought their own realtor into the sale (who I now had to pay). For this reason, I would put in 0.5% or 1%, or even 0% co-broke commission when you list online. A

small percentage might help keep a buyer who really wants to work with their realtor, but saves you paying a lot to a realtor who did not help bring the buyer to you. Most buyers search on their own online for homes and the realtor doesn't direct them. It's unlikely their realtor would steer them towards a For Sale By Owner. If needed, you can negotiate the commission if you get an offer. Since a lot of buyer's realtors, in response to the new real estate commissions rules, are requiring buyers to sign a contract that the buyer's will pay their fee, you may be off the hook for that.

- Fair housing laws require that you don't specify people or types of people to target when selling your home.
- Writing up your house description is an important piece of marketing your home. Pay it close attention, evoking as many pleasant feelings as possible, and pointing out the things you loved about your home and location. The pictures and this description are the work of marketing of your home, and it's what you would pay a realtor for, marketing the house. Do the best job with these that you can, as it's what draws buyers to your home.
- Disclose problems with your home. Talk to your real estate lawyer if you have a question about this. Paying for an inspection can head off nasty surprises later and might prevent a sale falling through. Giving the report to potential buyers can be a selling point.
- It's not over until the sale is closed. But problems with a sale falling through are not because you are

For Sale By Owner; it happens in sales involving realtors, too.

- Realtors don't sell homes for more when you adjust for the average home price sold. That claim is just a misleading way that the National Association of Realtors reports the average house prices of realtor-assisted verses FSBO sales. Find the 2007 study here: https://www.econstor.eu/bitstream/10419/38634/1/574941975.pdf
- The National Association of Realtors reports that 11% of homeowners do For Sale By Owner, but that doesn't count the 10% of owners who place their home in the MLS for a flat fee. Instead, those are counted as realtor-assisted sales. In reality, the percentage of people who sell without a realtor is closer to 20%.

Chapter Six

BUYING WITHOUT A REALTOR - IMPORTANT ADVICE

UPDATE IN RESPONSE TO THE NEW REAL ESTATE COMMISSIONS RULE, ENACTED AUGUST 2024

Since writing this book, the NAR (National Association of Realtors) has settled a lawsuit that resulted in a new rules for how realtors are compensated, and an advantage of being self-published is that I can update this book, so you'll know how this affects both buyers and sellers. In this chapter, focusing on advice for buyers.

In the past, the commissions were charged to the seller of the home, paid to their real estate agent at closing. That agent split that commission with a buyer's broker, if there was an agent representing the buyer. And when I learned about real estate brokers, I learned that those agents split their half with the agency or brokerage that they operate out of, the company that had the physical real estate company office.

But in August of 2024, the new real estate commissions rules went into effect. Sellers are no longer expected to pay both realtors, as has traditionally been the practice for most of the US. If you've read this entire book, you've seen at least one example of where a realtor who was supposed to be acting in the best interest of the buyers gave me information that helped make the sale, but exposed private information about the buyer's finances. A buyer's agent wants the deal to happen, so they get paid. It has long struck me as a conflict of interest that the seller is the one who pays the buyer's agent, and I'm glad the laws have changed.

Though maybe hasn't changed as much as we might hope. The seller will be informed and offered the opportunity to decide: do they want to pay both agents, or just the agent who is marketing their home? I expect that most will agree to continue to pay both agents, at least at first. I also expect that their realtors will strongly recommend that they do, in order to entice the buyer's realtors to come see the home, as the seller will guarantee that they will be paid.

I've already seen ads that say "No showings without a qualified buyer's agent!" Wording that wasn't necessary before the new rules. The agents are striving for the current system to stay the same. And, when I called about a property and accidentally interfaced with a realtor from Zillow, and not the seller's realtor, I was told I couldn't see the house without a realtor representing me. Which should not be true unless the seller has specified that in the contract. I pushed back, and they said they weren't a licensed realtor yet, but one would call me and explain the rules to me. I never received that call.

In the case of buying, you may have been working with a realtor, and now that the real estate commission rules have changed, that realtor may be asking for you to sign a contract that says that you will pay them their fee at closing if the seller refuses to. This may be a shock as that fee was always paid by the seller, and you may not have budgeted a realtor's fee into your expense for buying a home. If you continue to use a realtor, know that you can offer a little less on a home if you have to pay the realtor, and in essence, that is the seller paying this fee out of their proceeds. If you are going to continue to use a realtor, make sure that any contract you sign has an end date, or is for exactly the one home you want to look at, that you can end the contract when you wish, and that if you find a home without your realtor's help, that you aren't require to pay them a commission. You don't want to lock yourself into a contract and then do all the work yourself with finding a home, and still be required to pay them a fee of many thousands of dollars. Read the contracts carefully.

But if instead you'd like to avoid signing those contracts and navigate buying on your own without a realtor, the ability to search for homes online is extensive. And, as you'll see in this chapter, you'll it might put you at an advantageous position as it did when I bought my condos, as I approached the seller's realtors on properties without a realtor to represent me.

In both cases, I believe we had the seller's realtor working on my side, *even thought they explicitly told me they were only representing the seller.* But I think both were instrumental in getting my offers accepted, because the selling realtor *knew* that if we had the winning bids, that *they got double commissions.*

With the new real estate commissions rules, that might not be the case, the realtor may not get *any* additional monies for selling to a buyer without a broker.

BUT - *the seller will!* So if you come to the table with an offer and a seller has agreed to pay both realtors, it will be a sweeter offer for them if they don't have to pay your realtor. This may still be the advantage that can win you the property in a seller's market.

Here's the story of how I ended up ditching the use of a realtor to help me buy a home.

SEARCHING FOR A REALTOR TO HELP WITH A SEARCH

Once I sold my last home, I was looking to invest in a home. But moving was so exhausting, I rented a place to live for a year, giving myself breathing room for a search. I soon needed to reinvest my house equity because rent is so expensive and buying (with my equity down payment) was the only way I could afford to live in the region where I do and not use up my equity paying rent.

I started searching on Zillow.com, but it was overwhelming. I didn't narrow my search by town; I was open to an extensive region around my work. I was considering both single and multi-family homes. I contacted a friend who is a realtor who gave me advice about buying multi-family property and offered to find me a realtor who would work hard to find me one. She said a good realtor can sometimes find new properties. If they know owners who are looking to sell, they could set up a deal for me by communicating to owners they have a buyer interested in their property, even before it comes on the market. I was excited and happy to work with a realtor who was that good at their job, using their knowledge and contacts to help me, who knew my criteria and would do the search for me. I met with the person she recommended, and we spoke for over an hour about what I wanted, what I like, the pre-approval terms for my mortgage I had to work within, the towns I like, where I work, etc. I was grateful to pass the responsibility of my home search off to her. I didn't sign a buyer-broker agreement right away, as I wanted to give her a trial run and see if our personalities matched and how good she would be at finding properties I liked. A realtor may encourage you to sign a buyer-broker agreement before they show you a home and reassure you the seller pays them, especially with the new rules enacted in 2024. But be cautious about signing any legal contract, read it carefully, and know what your rights are. In particular, ***you want to keep the right to find homes on your own, and if you do, you shouldn't have to pay a realtor's fee.***

Instead of working hard on my behalf the way my friend described, the realtor set up a daily email that contained properties that met my basic search criteria. When I clicked on the link in the email, it took me to her company's website for browsing the real estate listings. Their website was hard to navigate compared to Zillow.com or Trulia.com, and I'd take the addresses from her email and paste it into one of my preferred real estate searching websites, allowing me to browse pictures that were a decent size and see immediately on a map where the property was.

EMAIL NOTIFICATIONS OF REAL ESTATE LISTINGS – NOT ENOUGH!

I could have set up and saved a similar search (you can too) and received an automated email of properties matching real estate criteria in Zillow or any of the real estate search sites. You can receive emails immediately, or daily, notifying you about new listings.

The email notifications my realtor set up for me wasn't the help with my search I was looking for. Anyone can get sorted properties emailed to them every day by drawing a region (so multiple towns), by town, by home type (in my case, multi-family), by price range, by For Sale By Owner, by size requirements, by amenity (a garage, etc.), or any combination of search criteria. You can specify exactly what you are looking for and the software will search and notifying you. When you do this have the software notify you immediately so you find out right away when a property comes on the market.

Occasionally, the realtor would call and ask if I wanted to go see any of the homes. One day I opened her email and saw a perfect (for my specifications) — and rare — two-family home, that was in a location close to my work, and well within my budget. I called the realtor when I saw the email, first thing on a Saturday morning, about 15 hours after the property "went live." By the time she returned my call, other buyers had already booked the property with showings for that day, and the owner ended up taking an offer before I even got to see it.

Instead of clueing me in on a property that was about to come on the market, giving me an advantage, my realtor was sending out an automated email that I didn't see for 15 hours after it listed. Quite the opposite level of service than I expected.

Disappointed, I told the realtor that if emailing was all she would do to help me find a home, I wouldn't be using her services. She should have been on top of the search so that the instant that property came on the market, *she called me*. Instead, 15 hours in (and too late), *I* pointed it out to *her*. If I work with a realtor to show me properties, I want them invested in my search, finding and informing me of properties that work as soon as they come on the market. That's the work they would do to earn their commission. And with the new rules, that work might have to be paid for by me, the buyer.

After that discouraging experience I probably should have

gone back to trusting my own instincts and dropped the idea of using a realtor. But I was still tired, working a lot, and ever optimistic that someone else might be able to help me.. So, I called another realtor recommended by a friend who had the reputation of being one of the most active and successful realtors in a town I was looking in. I started looking at properties with him but I ended up feeling uncomfortable with some "jokes" this realtor made, talk that became too personal as he inquired over and over about my dating life, and eventually, one joke that crossed the line. He also let a condominium slip under contract to someone else, not once, but twice, because he'd failed to follow up quickly and get information I requested about the property, I never got to make an offer. I felt very disempowered by his conversation, besides the fact that he wasn't taking my search seriously. Months later, I had a conversation with him about the situation and he said, "I'm sorry you were offended. That's just how I talk to all my friends. Everyone I work with knows that's my sense of humor, which is often inappropriate. I shouldn't have assumed we were close enough friends that I could joke around. I should have kept it strictly professional." Of course he should have kept it professional. I was no longer comfortable working with him.

HOW TO SEARCH REAL ESTATE WITHOUT A REALTOR

Disappointed in both experiences, I searched without a realtor's help, without the help of a "buyer broker."

I started going to open houses (usually hosted by the listing realtor) and searching online myself. The listing agents at open houses were always surprised to learn that I wasn't working with a realtor. But it was excellent news for them. If I bought, they wouldn't have to split a commission with a buyer's agent.

In addition, I've been told that realtors don't expect to sell homes at open houses. Instead, it's a good opportunity for them to build their client base. All the hosting agents would give me contact information and try to sell me on their services as a buyer broker. Given my history, I was no longer interested.

I set up my own searches, and had the real estate sites email me *immediately* when homes came on the market that were in my price range, desired location, and that fit my other criteria. Remember, you can have the sites email you once a week, once a day, or immediately. You might get a lot more email than you like, but I recommend you get listing the instant they go live.

When I saw a property I liked, I'd find out *who the listing broker was,* and contact *them* about seeing the house as soon as possible.

HOW TO DEAL WITH THE LISTING AGENT ONLY

Finding out who the listing agent is takes some work because realtors pay for advertising space on real estate sites. So the first realtor listed ***is not necessarily the listing agent.*** The first realtor listed has often paid to have that place on the page.

If you don't have a realtor working on your behalf, contact the listing broker directly, because the full commission (paid by the owner) is paid to the listing realtor.

Or now, with the new real estate commissions laws, if you don't have a realtor working for you, you are saving the seller a bunch of money! This will make your offer more attractive for the realtor and they might help convince the owner to take your offer, or will be more attractive to the seller if they had expected to pay your realtor. If you call on a property and talk to a realtor, ask if they are the listing agent and, if not, keep asking until you find them. Sometimes the real estate sites will label the listing broker, making it easier for you to contact them directly.

The next two sections describe purchases where I think it made a difference for me to be working directly with the seller's agent, and the examples will guide you on how to do it confidently.

BIDDING ON A BANK-OWNED PROPERTY

I was looking at properties in my town and saw a condo come on the market at around $30,000 under the market price. It was bank owned. I called (and called and called) the realtor. It was very hard to reach him at first. I'm sure his phone was ringing off the hook, because the price was ridiculously low. I didn't believe that I'd get the property, as I knew there'd be a lot of competition because it was a bargain. When the listing realtor showed me the condo, I learned they would sell it in a week. Everyone interested had to submit best and final offers by 5:00 p.m. the following Monday. When the listing realtor realized I didn't have a realtor working with me, he told me several times he was representing the bank, and couldn't help me, as he had to act in their best interest, not mine. I understood this to be the case, and if you find yourself in this position, no matter how nice the realtor, remember, they are working only for the person who hired them.

I was eager to get the condo. It was in a pleasant area, walkable to a grocery store. Behind it was a soccer field with trees and a playground. It needed updating badly, but nothing needed doing right away. It was livable and I'm handy. Though the realtor didn't give me any inside information, he gave me some gentle guidance about where he thought my bid needed to be, and I submitted my offer.

At the last minute a couple bids came in higher, and the listing realtor called me and asked if I wanted to change my bid. I suspected the reason he was trying to help guide my bid was that *he knew if I got the condo he got the full commission.* The other bids were being submitted by realtors on behalf of clients. So if I was the one to buy the condo, it meant more money in his pocket. I increased my bid, and I got the property.

Once I won the bid, I had the lawyer who helped me sell my house as a For Sale By Owner take look at the offer letter and the purchase and sale before I signed, because without a realtor to represent me, I wanted to be sure I wasn't signing something that wouldn't allow an inspection or contained anything else that might surprise me. It didn't take her long to review the documents, and we did this all over email. The offer letters and subsequent purchase and sale were standard and she's very familiar with them.

I had now purchased this condo without the help of a realtor working for me, for about $30,000 under market price. I'll never know if it motivated the selling realtor to give me guidance on both my initial offer, and the last minute nudge to up my bid, because he didn't have to share his commission with a realtor working on my end, but I suspect it may have been the case.

MAKING AN OFFER TO THE LISTING REALTOR AFTER AN OPEN HOUSE

The next condo I bought I applied the same strategy. This time I attended an open house, as the listing broker is usually the one hosting it. Once I knew it interested me, I asked the agent at the open house how I make an offer, and she said, "Have your realtor write up an offer," assuming that I was working with a realtor, even though I didn't have one with me.

When I told her I didn't have one, she seemed more interested. She said she would email me what the offer should comprise. I filled out that offer form and sent it back to her, and within 24 hours I had an accepted offer.

Perhaps she encouraged the buyer to take my offer because I was working without a realtor, because I got offer accepted pronto, and at a great price, though they'd had a previous offer fall through and were eager to sell it. But I believe the fact that I came without an agent helped me to get my offer accepted quickly. When a realtor doesn't have to share their commission with a buyer-broker, it doubles their commission earned on a property.

Again, with the new real estate commissions rules, this saving of commissions won't go to the seller's realtor (unless the have this agreement in the contract with the seller). But, instead, you are potentially saving the seller the amount that would normally be paid to a buyer's realtor. It's logical to assume that this would motivate the the seller to sell to you, and if there are multiple offers, could definitely get yours on the top when the purchase price and costs are calculated.

I once again had my real estate lawyer review contracts for a very nominal fee, just for my own piece of mind.

BIDDING WARS

Lately, realtors have been trying to generate bidding wars for houses by listing lower than market price and then requiring that all "best and final offers" are submitted by a deadline. I think this is a dangerous game for a homeowner, even if it might generate enough interest to get a bidding war going. It's an easier strategy for a realtor, because if it works, they sell the home in a week, wrapping up their work on selling the house quickly. But to list way under market price? What if no one makes a higher offer? It would be awkward to adjust the price upwards after. At the moment, the market where I live is a seller's market. Buyers are desperate, which is why these invented auctions are working.

It's tough for the buyer; being outbid stinks. If you take part in bidding on a home, have your lawyer ready to check your offer. Perhaps, if you are presenting an offer without a realtor, the seller's broker will help push your offer to the front, or perhaps the seller themselves will ask their realtor to take a smaller commission if they know they don't have to pay your realtor, and with the new rules on commissions, the seller will already know that they will get more money in their pocket by not having to pay a realtor on your behalf.

SUBMITTING A WELL-WRITTEN LETTER WITH YOUR OFFER

My advice in previous chapters about doing a careful job writing the copy for your house description can also apply to buying. You want to evoke emotion and paint a clear picture of all reasons you want this home, and how you will cherish it, how you expect to enjoy living there.

If you are submitting an offer, or engaged in a bidding war, it's not unusual for a buyer to submit a letter to the owners summarizing why they want to buy the home. Owners can be sentimental about their homes, especially if they've been there a long time, raised a family in the home, built it themselves or made extensive improvements. They may want it to go to someone who will appreciate their home and the work they put into it, and a letter stating warmly and sincerely how you envision loving the home might give you the edge over another buyer or get the home for a better price. If you bid all you can, but it's lower than the bid of someone who didn't write a letter, you might still win the bidding if the owner wants an invested caretaker to be the new owner of their cherished home.

You should write the letter to evoke emotion. Listing facts, like, "This is a reasonable commute to my work" won't motivate a seller! Instead, paint an emotional picture of how you imagine yourself living in the home. If it aligns with what the owners hope will be the legacy of their home, your letter might sway them to accept your offer. For example, something like this might be a more heartfelt, persuasive expression of why you want to live in a particular home:

"Buying this home will allow me to spend more time with my family, as it's close to my work. I can't wait to push my kids on the swing in the oak tree in the backyard, and I can imagine us eating brunch out on the screened porch. I feel like this would be an amazing place to raise happy children. We love the decorating and the warmth throughout the home. We look forward to tending the gardens, growing vegetables, and having fresh-cut flowers from the perennial beds."

So if there are qualities about the home that are unique, or that the homeowners added — something about the location or neighborhood you love, or decorating that you admire, or landscaping that you look forward to enjoying (that's a labor of love for many homeowners), *anything* that makes the owner feel that you truly *see and appreciate* the things they love about their home — point those out in your letter. Let the seller know they are turning their beloved home over to someone who appreciates its finer characteristics and will care for it.

HOW TO SAVE WHEN BUYING: SEARCH FOR FOR SALE BY OWNER HOMES SPECIFICALLY

Don't be put off by a For Sale By Owner, as a matter of fact, you might do well to search them out. An online search for "For Sale By Owner" in whatever site you use to find real estate will bring them up, unless they are flat-fee listings in MLS, in which case, it will be harder to tell if they are For Sale By Owner. Zillow now lists For Sale By Owner under it's own tab, you have to explicitly choose it over agent represented homes. Or, it may be a drop-down menu. Because Zillow has made it harder for For Sale By Owner homes, some sellers now list with an agent in what's known as a flat-fee listing.

If you aren't using a realtor, the most important task is to find out who the listing realtor is. Ask when you call on a property if the realtor you are speaking with is the listing broker. If they aren't, keep going until you are speaking with the listing broker. If the home is a flat-fee listing, *the listing broker should give you the contact information for the owner*. At least, that's how it's supposed to work.

Once you find a home you like that is For Sale By Owner, go to those open houses or contact the owners on your own and do so without a realtor. Though, please keep safety in mind, and use common sense when going to a stranger's home, if you are on your own, ask a friend or relative to go with you.

Owners will often have open houses for you to view the property, but if it's a home you love, and the market is competitive, set up a showing yourself as soon as possible. I have a friend who listed her condominium and waited a week before having her first open house. A woman contacted her, she showed the property once, and it went under agreement. If you've set up a search to notify you of new properties and see one you like, move quickly. By setting up an appointment for a showing with the owner, you might beat the rush or competition of an open house and perhaps avoid a bidding war. Sellers love nothing more than to sell their home quickly.

If you hear stories about owners who sell on their own being hard to deal with, consider the source of that information. Both realtors — and people who've paid big commissions to realtors — want to believe that using a realtor is the best and only way to buy and sell homes. But for those of us who have bought or sold without realtors, we no longer see a reason to do it any other way. On occasions when a homeowner is hard to deal with or has overpriced their home, you can always walk away or manage the process through lawyers. Selling For Sale By Owner is becoming increasingly common, as 10-20% of sales are FSBO, so don't limit your search to only homes that listed with realtors. And, if you hire a realtor to help you do your home search, make sure that the contract states that if you find a For Sale By Owner home all on your own, that you may purchase it without you — or the seller — having to pay your agent.

WHY YOU'LL SAVE WITH FOR SALE BY OWNER

I think most buyers who approached me when I did For Sale By Owner knew I had more flexibility in price because I didn't have a realtor, and you, as a buyer, can keep that in mind, too. The money saved by not paying a real estate agent doesn't have to land solely in the seller's pockets; it can be a better deal for both sides. Sometimes owners get sentimental about their homes and expect to get top dollar and won't budge. But more likely you'll find homeowners who are reasonable and know that holding onto the home for months longer is more expensive than coming down some on price. It's all about a win-win and finding the right price for the market. When I didn't hire a realtor, I knew I could be much more flexible on price, and so I was willing to accept less for my home. I always ended up with more in my pocket than if I'd hired a realtor.

WHEN TO CONSIDER HIRING A LAWYER

If you have a problem with an unpleasant owner but really want the home, try to have communication happen through lawyers, or at least, hire one on your side. Get an estimate of the cost of this up front or hire the lawyer for a flat fee. And though email can take away some of the discomfort of face-to-face offers and counter-offers, ask if your lawyer will handle the price negotiations if you feel uncomfortable doing so with an owner.

Your mortgage attorney for your bank — usually paid for you as part of closing costs — has parallel interests to yours, so hiring your own attorney may not be necessary, at least not for things like title search. They won't start their work, though, until you have a signed purchase and sale agreement. You can hire a lawyer to look over your offer letter and purchase and sale document, which shouldn't require much time on their part.

If you are a confident buyer, you can always do this yourself, but make sure you read contracts documents carefully. Most are standard documents, meaning everyone uses a set template, but that doesn't mean you shouldn't give it a very careful read. A satisfactory home inspection is often a contingency of the deal; if you hire an inspector and they discover big problems with the home, you can walk away from the deal and have your deposit returned to you in full. For myself, though I feel like I could have understood the contracts, I always felt a little safer having my real estate lawyer take a look before I signed. They have a lot more education and experience than I do.

When you make an initial offer, give it an expiration date — usually 24 hours. You don't want to be hung up on this property if it doesn't work out.

NEGOTIATING COMMISSIONS

It's possible you can use the fact that there is only one realtor to pay in price negotiations, buying or selling. Say you and the seller are close to a deal, but you've run out of money for upping your offer. You can suggest that the realtor take a smaller commission to make up the difference. The seller's realtor only expected to make half of the commission, as most deals have a realtor working with the buyer and one working for the seller, so you may be able to use that to your advantage, and ask if they will make up the difference by lowering the commission rate they receive at closing. Or with the new real estate commissions rules, you can remind the seller that you are not using a realtor, and they won't need to pay one for you, and it can sweeten the pot for your offer.

NEGOTIATING A LOWER COMMISSION WITH FOR SALE BY OWNER

When I listed as a For Sale By Owner in the MLS (Multiple Listing Service) with a flat-fee listing, it appeared as though the realtor who I'd paid to put my listing in was my realtor. The MLS didn't allow me to put "For Sale By Owner" anywhere in my description. So when a buyer looked at my home listing and would see realtor's contact info on my page, they probably figured there wasn't any reason they shouldn't bring their own realtor. And that's exactly what happened. People would come to my open houses with their realtors. Or, they'd come to the open house by themselves and then, when they wanted to make an offer, I'd find out they were working with a realtor.

I ended up having to pay for the realtor that represented my buyers, even though the realtor had done *nothing* to help with the sale of my home. When the buyers submitted their offer, my first counter-offer included not only a negotiated purchase price for the buyers, it also included a request for the realtor to drop her commission from 2.5% to 2%. She readily agreed, as she would still make $18,000 for writing up the offer letter for the buyers, and handling the back and forth of negotiating a price for them. I had put into my listing that I would co-broke with realtors at 2.5%, which is half of the going rate of real estate commissions in my area, the same they'd make on any home sale when they split with another realtor. I expected to pay this if a *realtor brought me a buyer*, but since *the buyer brought the realtor*, I didn't think it was too much to ask for the realtor to reduce her fee.

The buyers could also have requested that their realtor reduce her commission and not waited for me to make that request. The lower the commission I would have to pay, the more attractive the offer is to me, because it's less money out of my pocket. Since the buyers had done all the legwork up to that point (in finding the home online, going to the open house, and visiting the house again, twice), I think it would have been reasonable for them to ask if the realtor would submit an offer on their behalf that included reduced realtor's commission.

REMEMBER, THE LISTING BROKER IS WORKING FOR THE SELLER

If you contact the listing broker, remember that person is working for the seller, and *not for you.* If you feel more comfortable having a real estate agent who is a buyer broker, you can bring one into the negotiation. That's the way it works for most real estate transactions.

FIRST-TIME BUYER SAVINGS

Though this has nothing to do with working without a realtor, I wanted to mention that a buyer looking to purchase real estate can save if they are buying a home for the first time, because there are special financing options available only to first-time buyers, and sometimes, low income homes that are only available for purchase by first time home buyers.

Saving a 20% down payment on a property with real estate prices where they are can be an impossible hurdle for those looking to buy for the first time. So some banks offer first-time buyers a mortgage with as little as a 3% down payment, and sometimes with 0% down!

If you are lucky enough to have someone willing to gift you a down payment, the mortgage company may be okay with that as long as you get a letter saying it is a gift, and not a loan. This is another way for you to get into a home that you wouldn't otherwise be able to afford.

Search for "first time home buyer" education courses in your area for details or contact your bank for a mortgage company. I really admire and appreciate that there are organizations doing that work, because having a home of your own brings safety, security, and happiness to us and our family, and connection to our community.

CHAPTER 6 BOTTOM LINE

- Realtors that do an active search of homes for you are great, and worth working with, and if you want to work with a realtor, search for one who will do that work, and don't sign a contract until you are sure you found them. But, setting up a daily email of new listings is something you can do yourself with any online real estate site. If you do so, I'd suggest getting notified immediately when a property matching your criteria comes on the market, and move quickly so as not to lose the home.
- A comfortable working relationship with a realtor means they keep things professional. Don't accept anything less; again, their job is to seek out a home you'll be happy with and help you get it under contract, not to socialize with you. Remember, this is a business transaction.
- If you do want to search with a realtor, know that now that the real estate commission rules have changed, that you will likely be required to sign a contract before they will work with you, and that you may be on the hook for their commission if the seller isn't offering to pay your agent. Read your contract carefully, and only hire representation if the agent can help you on a specific property, instead of a blanket contract that entitles them to a fee even if you find the

property yourself, like at an open house without them present.

- **Seek out the listing broker on a property by calling and asking, or by attending open houses which are usually hosted by the seller's agent.**
- Buying a bank-owned property saved me money, and it may have been the fact that I didn't have a realtor that caused the seller's realtor to push the deal through quickly.
- If you decide to submit offers in a bidding war, consider having a real estate lawyer check over the offer letter. This could protect you in the event you learn something unacceptable about the property that makes you decide to pull out of the deal after winning the bid.
- If a realtor knows you don't have a realtor working with you, they might encourage a seller to accept your offer over others.
- If the seller has agreed, due to the new real estate commission rule of 2024 to pay the buyer's agent, if you don't have an agent, they might be more inclined to accept your offer over others.
- **You can save money buying from an owner who is doing For Sale By Owner. Knowing that the seller isn't paying a real estate agent's commission gives you a hint that that enables them to be more flexible on price, as long as you don't bring a realtor into the process.** Unfortunately, these are harder to find as many For Sale By Owner are doing listings for a flat fee to get into the MLS. But if you find one, good for you, don't shy away as you can

both save money now, as neither of you are paying am agent!

- Having a real estate attorney handle the offer letter, purchase and sale document, and price negotiations is a good way to feel confident about purchasing without a realtor, or buying from a For Sale By Owner. There is always an attorney working on behalf of the bank, if you are getting a mortgage, so there is a lawyer who's looking out for the bank's interests, and by default, yours.
- Finding out who the listing real estate agent is on any property you want to buy will make you an attractive buyer. The selling agent gets double commission, and may encourage the seller to accept your offer over the offers of other buyers. Keep asking until you find the seller's agent. The new real estate commissions rules means that the seller saves this money, making your offer more appealing.
- Writing is important, and if you write a personal, well-written letter to submit with your offer, it might help you get the home. Use feeling words, evoke sentimental emotion. Express how much you love the home, pointing out qualities of the home that the seller has pride in and that you will appreciate when you make it your own home.
- **If you are a first-time buyer, be sure to check out special deals on homes for first-time buyers, or financing for your situation.**

Chapter Seven

WHAT YOU SHOULD KNOW IF YOU USE A REALTOR TO BUY

REAL ESTATE BROWSING WAS ONCE ONLY IN A REALTOR'S OFFICE

Property listing and advertising has changed a lot in the years since I owned my first house. Back then, realtors restricted access to the Multiple Listing Service (MLS) to realtors only. If you wanted to browse houses and the relevant details about properties, you had to go into an office and work with a realtor. They would place a huge binder of listing sheets before you on a desk where you searched by town to find homes. If there was a property you wanted to see, the realtor would contact the listing broker, or the seller, and make arrangements to take you to see the house. The listing broker would hold the keys at their office.

REALTORS BECAME EXPERTS IN THEIR REGION

In those earlier days, realtors were aware of new properties being added to the book and often specialized in a certain town and knew every property that came on the market. Even today, they still attend “realtor open houses” showing a newly-listed property to other realtors during a weekday so they can get a sense of the home, learn about its features before showing it to their clients, and also network with other realtors.

If you see a realtor open house sign and are interested in the property, stop in — they are open to the public, too. Not only will you have a look at a property new to the market, the realtors often entice each other to come see the property by serving food, so you can get snacks, too!

ALL REAL ESTATE IS NOW VIEWABLE AND SEARCHABLE ONLINE

Today, realtors list all the houses in the MLS online, and then they’re picked up by real estate sites like Zillow.com. Owners can also bypass the MLS and list directly in Zillow.com and other real estate listing sites (which I recommend). Buyers can browse pictures and listing details to their heart’s content. And instead of searching by town, they can search on many criteria. When a buyer finds a property they want to see in person, they have two options. They can request a showing through the real estate listing site they are using to search properties. A realtor, who has paid to advertise their services on that site, will get the contact information of the potential buyer and then arrange a showing with the seller’s realtor. Alternately, if the buyer already has a realtor they are working with, they’ll call them with the address and ask them to arrange a showing.

REAL ESTATE COMMISSIONS AND WHO PAYS

Once the purchase and sale document has been signed by both parties, the real estate agent's work marketing the home is over. They may help you further to make sure the property closes and they get their commission. It is the lawyer's job now to make sure all is done properly and legally, that a clean title to the home will be delivered at closing. A real estate agent can be very knowledgeable about the laws, but that isn't their job; their job is *marketing.*

There are usually two realtors working on a deal — one who represents the seller (the listing agent), and one representing the buyers. Most often a buyer has a realtor that helps them see all the houses they are interested in, as they can gain access through lockboxes and show the home without the listing realtor being present.

In the past, sellers paid both agents, usually out of a chunk of equity that they get from selling the home.

When the sale is complete, the two agents will split the commission, each getting half. Then the agents also share the commission with their broker, the real estate professional who owns and runs the office the agent works at.

With the new real estate commissions rules enacted in 2024, the seller is not required to pay the buyer's real estate agent, and this will be negotiated on every house listing and between each buyer and their agent.

If you choose to continue to pay both creators, you can pay up to 6% commission, but another way to save money is to research discount brokers who charge less. A real estate agent might advise you that agents will try harder to sell a house where they will make a 3% commission (their half of the 6%) rather than on one where they will only make 2.5% or less. They will want you to pay the full 6% commission to motivate realtors, but commissions are negotiable.

Back in the days when real estate agents held exclusive access to the big MLS books and realtors who knew the market and inventory did most of the searching, it might have been more important to pay the full commission. You didn't want a real estate agent to avoid telling a buyer about your house because selling them a different house in town would earn them an additional 1%, or because they are the listing broker on that other house and they want to keep both sides of the commission.

Today, buyers are looking online for houses and a real estate agent can't hide a house that a buyer wants to see. Buyers can easily search for, discover, and decide they want to see any home that is for sale.

MAKE SURE YOUR CONTRACT DOESN'T PROHIBIT YOU FROM BUYING WITHOUT A REALTOR

If you are working with a realtor to look for homes and you have a pleasant working relationship with them, that's great. And if you have signed a contract that states the realtor is working for you as a buyer broker, and you will pay them for that service, then you know for certain they are working in your best interest.

If you've signed an agreement with a buyer broker but the seller, when the house is sold, is the one who will pay your real estate agent, then it is in that realtor's and the seller's best interest, financially, to close the deal. A realtor is trying to earn a commission, and as a buyer, you need to keep in mind their motivation.

If you work with a real estate agent to show you homes, *make sure that there isn't any language in your contract that will prevent you from buying a home without them.* If you find a home on your own, such as For Sale By Owner homes or other homes that you discover without their help (e.g., homes found through a friend or relative), make sure it is excluded from your agreement with the real estate agent.

In addition, now that the real estate commission has changed the rules as to who pay realtors, and sellers are no longer expected to pay the buyer's realtor, some realtors are getting more stringent in having prospective buyers sign a buyer broker agreement up front, before they show them any homes.

This is understandable, as agents sometimes spend hours and days and months showing a prospective buyer property, with the understanding that they will get a commission once they find a house. But what if they never do, or what if the seller of that chosen house has decided they aren't going to pay a buyer's realtor? Buyer's agents are trying to protect against this buy having buyers sign a buyer broker agreement that says that the buyer will pay them their commission if the seller doesn't. Most buyers, trying to maximize their buying power, will find this hard to afford, and why I'm putting out a separate book on how to buy without a realtor, and have updated my chapter on that in this book.

Some realtors won't work with a For Sale By Owner, while others will take the initiative and negotiate a fee with the owner themselves. Realtors are only entitled to a commission if they, in fact, are the ones who find you a home they think you will like and then take you to see it, or if they work with you and the owner of a house you've found to make a sale happen.

WHEN AN AGENT MIGHT NOT BE ACTING IN YOUR BEST INTEREST

A buyer's agent once confided in me during a price negotiation that although the buyers had presented an offer as their "best and final," they could offer more, and would, but only if I would come down some first. She even let me know how much more they qualified for with the bank.

If I was that buyer, I'd be furious. The agent was trying to help me out and make the deal happen for her clients, but I wondered if the buyer had any idea that their realtor was giving me a peek at their sensitive financial information. I know the buyers considered this "their" realtor. Be cognizant of the fact that realtors are looking to close the deal. Perhaps when it works out that the deal goes through, and everyone gets what they want, it's fine, and that is probably the case in most real estate negotiations. But this is a cautionary tale to remind you that your buyer broker is looking to make their commission and close the deal. Keep that in mind if you are not the one paying them.

CHAPTER 7 BOTTOM LINE

- In the past, the only way to view homes was to go to a realtor's office and see the listings in a binder. Realtors were experts in their region and could help you find a home that suited your needs. Today, searching is open to all online. Since buyers know exactly what they are looking for and can set up their own searches, buyers are doing much of what used to be a real estate agent's job.

- Remember that, unless you are paying your realtor as a buyer-broker, the seller ultimately pays the realtor, and their goal is to make that commission. This doesn't always line up with acting in your best interest.
- If you are working with an agent, make sure your contract allows you to buy homes you find on your own — such as For Sale By Owner homes or homes you discover through contacts — free from having to pay a commission. Use a real estate lawyer to manage the sale at a much lower cost.
- An agent's commission is negotiable and there are discount brokerages that charge lower commissions.

Chapter Eight

FOR SALE BY OWNER CHECKLIST

If you would like to try doing For Sale By Owner, here is an ordered list of what I would tell a friend to help them sell their own home. More detailed instructions for each step follow.

1. **Hire a Real Estate Lawyer to Help You Navigate the Process**
2. **Clean Out and Fix Up**
3. **Take Pictures or Hire a Real Estate Photographer**
4. **Decide on a Price Based on Market Research or Hire an Appraiser**
5. **Prepare Marketing Materials**
6. **List Your House Online as For Sale By Owner**
7. **Schedule Open Houses on the Weekends by Thursday of Each Week**
8. **Submit Offers and Earnest Money to Your Attorney for Escrow, Sign P&S**

9. **Schedule an Inspection and Walk-through of your House**
10. **Prepare For and Attend Closing**

STEP ONE: HIRE A REAL ESTATE LAWYER TO HELP YOU NAVIGATE THE PROCESS

Your lawyer will provide forms, hold deposits in escrow, and arrange the closing. Ask for advice about disclosures.

I recommend using a real estate lawyer, because that's what's most common in my state.

In your state, there might a title company, a third-party company that provides real estate closing services. They focus in researching and verifying the ownership of a property. They help ensure that the property being sold has a clear and marketable title, free from any liens, judgments, or other encumbrances, and they can handle holding the escrow, prepare closing statements and oversee the closing. You might not even need a lawyer for much if there is a title company handling the sale. But in my state, I used a lawyer for all of this. Except the title search, which is required by the mortgage company, who hires a lawyer on behalf of the buyer, and this is paid for out of closing costs. If you aren't in Massachusetts, insure around as to how title transfer is done in your state. I know someone who sold for sale by owner in NH, the escrow was held at a title company and the closing was smooth and easy with a title company who were very expert at the process.

If you are hiring a real estate lawyer, you should be able to interview them either in person or over the phone and explain that you want to try selling your house yourself. Ask them if they have experience helping sellers who have done so, what they would charge for this service, and what it includes. You want someone who will:

- Provide you with standard forms (like blank offer forms)
- Prepare the purchase and sale document once you accept an offer
- Review any changes the buyer or their attorney or their realtor make to the purchase and sale agreement
- Set the timeline for closing (your lawyer should be familiar with how long it takes to secure financing, prepare the title, get inspections, etc.)
- Guide you in disclosure statements, if needed
- Guide you in preparing for closing, giving you a list and timeline of what you need to provide for closing (fire certificate, septic documents like title 5, 6D, etc.). Ask for a list with deadlines.
- Title preparation (ideally your attorney can be the title agent)
- Prepare documents for and attend closing (which may even take place in their office)

Your lawyer may also be willing to handle price negotiations with the buyers or their agent or attorney, which may make things less awkward if you are having trouble agreeing on a price, or if, after the inspection, you need to negotiate repairs or a price adjustment to compensate for problems. I was very grateful that my lawyer wasn't just willing to do this, she was good at it. She was authoritative and knowledgeable. Experience helps. My lawyer had been a realtor for many years before she became an attorney and was also once a teacher. So not only did she have an incredible knowledge of the process, she was also clear when explaining the steps to me. It's important to have a lawyer with whom you feel comfortable asking questions. I asked lots of questions, sometimes asking her to explain the same thing several times until I "got" it. Don't be embarrassed. There's a lot of paperwork and the entire process is cluttered with unfamiliar jargon, much of which we encounter only a few times in our lives when we are buying or selling our homes. Ask lots of questions and expect them to guide you through the process. And keep asking until you feel comfortable.

In all cases I paid the lawyer a flat fee, payable at closing out of the proceeds of the sale, not an hourly rate. I tried to be cognizant of the fact that my lawyer wasn't being paid by the hour and attempted to be reasonable about taking up her time. Your lawyer might have an upper limit of the hours for a fixed price, beyond which you might incur more charges. Make sure you find this out up front and know what the hourly rate beyond the set hours will be.

A friend of mine contacted a real estate lawyer who said they would charge her $250 an hour to represent her in her home sale. She said, "I'm more comfortable with one inclusive price. What would that be?" He responded with $850, which was very reasonable, and now she knows and can plan for exactly what her costs will be.

If there is a problem with your property, like lead paint, asbestos, a problem with the septic, or any other significant issue, ask your attorney about disclosure documents and have them help you do that process correctly and legally.

STEP TWO: CLEAN OUT AND FIX UP

You have to clean your house.

You know you have to clean your house, right?

You have to clean it *hard.*

Whether or not you hire a realtor, preparing a home to sell is the second hardest part of moving, the first being the packing and moving itself. And neither of these is something a realtor can help you with at all. So take a deep breath and start chucking the clutter.

You may think you can get the property on the market and then get rid of things. But the de-cluttering you do will help make your home more marketable. The first step in listing online is to get great pictures of your home, and your rooms will look larger and more pleasant if you de-clutter first.

For some of us, if we've lived in the home for years, this process can take months. I was preparing my home to sell for a year. Ideally you want to list your house in the spring, which is the hot real estate season, though people buy homes all year-round and some believe selling off season gives an advantage as there is less competition. If you are just beginning to think about selling your home, give yourself some lead time to get it ready.

Clean out personal items while you are marketing your home. You want the buyer to imagine themselves living in your home, not imagining you living there. Pictures of your relatives and your vacations are distracting from what you want the buyer to be looking at: the house. Pack up personal things.

The imaginary journey your buyer will take (where they picture themselves living in your home) starts with your online write-up. But it continues when they arrive at your home with the blank slate you show them.

I once saw an ad for a condo, and I as I clicked through the pictures I was overwhelmed with all the apple-themed decor. There were apple dishes, apple towels, apple curtains, apple soaps and apple tablecloths. In addition, there were lots and lots of family photos, including the most unusual I'd ever seen: in the master bedroom was a quilt with a picture of the happy family of four spread over the entire bed! I thought it was so funny, I downloaded the picture, I've never seen anything like it. It's the opposite of what you want to do when you sell your home. How can anyone picture themselves living in that bedroom, with the family smiling up at them from the bed? I was wondering, "Why all the apple things? Who's the collector? What are these people like? Well, I can see what they look like." My curiosity about the family distracted me completely from looking at the rooms and features of the condominium.

I'm not disparaging the family, by the way. I think a family with that much pride and affection for each other must be a lucky one to belong to. My mom was great, but she didn't have my picture on her bed, though maybe it's because I didn't buy her enough apple-themed items. On the other hand, my mother once mentioned that she loved swans, and for every Mother's Day, birthday and Christmas after that, she inevitably received a swan-themed-something from one of her seven kids. Back then you couldn't search online for a "swan-themed gift" and order it up; we had to search through gift shops (filled with the kinds of things you'll agonize over keeping when you are trying to de-clutter, pack and move). So we showed effort, but the profusion of swan items must've been annoying after a while. Perhaps the mom of the apple family suffered from a similar slip of the tongue, and this extra-loving family couldn't help but shower her with every apple-themed decorative thing ever made.

If this is you — the quilt person, the photo person, the swan person, or the apple person — here's your chance to get rid of it all for good! And if that thought horrifies you, then pack it up and save it for decorating your new space. Maybe just one little apple potholder, but box up the 1,127 other apple things. You want your home to look a little lived in and lovely, but generic, leaving room for new personalities to spread out.

You might think buyers will be able to imagine the house with their own furnishings, but creating a blank canvas to make this easier is an important part of marketing. You want them to imagine themselves in your space, and also, you want them to look at the home you're selling, not distract them from it with your belongings and pictures. I know when I've looked at homes I can't help looking at family photos. I'm curious about people; we all are. So put the family photos away and only leave sparse belongings and decor that highlight your home's spaces. If you can't live without your photos, perhaps put them in a box under the bed for showings, and pull them back out when buyers have gone.

Empty your house. The more you get rid of, the more spacious and large your rooms will look, and that's good. Completely empty is not desirable, though, empty homes are harder to sell, perhaps because with no furniture it's harder for a buyer to imagine themselves living there. I suggest donating items because it's faster. You can try to sell them, but I didn't for a few reasons. First, as a single woman, it was a safety issue. I didn't want to have strangers coming to my home to look at items when I was alone. Second, it wasn't worth my time. I estimated how much time I would spend writing an ad, answering emails or phone calls to arrange a time to show the item, waiting while they decide whether to buy it and then load it in their vehicle. I didn't want to be doing that alone, so I had the added complexity of having a friend be there when someone came to see my item for sale. It usually added up to at least 2-4 hours I'd be spending and unless I was getting over $200 for the item, I decided it wasn't worth it. I also had so much else to do, and showing items for sale often took place on the weekend when I really had to be doing yard work, repairs, or other important things.

I never had a yard sale that made enough money that it was worth the time and trouble to move everything out to the yard, price each item, and then clean it back up after. If you live on a busy road and think this will work, though, go for it. A blanket or tarp with a sign saying "free" at the yard sale (or anytime) makes things disappear like magic; move items over there if it looks like they won't be selling. There are charities that will come and take everything for a set price, and there are organizations that take drop-off donations for free. That's what I did; I loaded the car week after week and took clothes, toys, and household goods to the local charity. It felt great, and I kept things out of landfills. I couldn't bring myself to get a dumpster. It made it a lot easier for me to part with items I didn't want to keep when I imagined someone else might get it and happily enjoy it, rather than throwing it in the trash. This also helps motivate my kids to donate, telling them they can donate the toys to another child. I have a very hard time throwing out something that was perfectly good. Donating was more motivating, and I de-cluttered better and faster. And people will take almost anything for free. If you get stuck with something you can't move yourself, see if someone wants it for free and let them transport it. The Freecycle website is a terrific way to do this.

I recommend reading *The Life-Changing Magic of Tidying*

Up, The Japanese Art of Decluttering and Organizing by Marie Kondo. Her advice on how to declutter is known as the Konmari Method. The book's method is a little extreme, but the basic question, "Does this bring me joy?" is a super-helpful guideline to use when deciding whether to keep an item. That moment of decision is so hard, and this book helps you get over that hump. I have to say that as I sat with item after item, even though an item gave me joy when I received it as a gift, or might bring me joy someday, or was once very useful but hadn't been so for years, asking "Does this bring me joy?" *in the present* helped clarify whether I should keep it. And once it went into the donate box, oh, the relief! It's so strange, because one moment I was agonizing over it, but then, decision made, I was so happy to let it go. Maybe it takes that brief goodbye ceremony to let go of things we have found useful or loved in our past. It can be so soothing, though, to give to others. You'll feel freer. If you struggle with this, please check out the book.

Think "simplify." Think minimalism. It's all good, and it'll be easier to move, too! On the slim chance you regret later getting rid of something, well, you can replace most items. But you'll probably never think about it again. If you are still agonizing over the decision, check out how much it would cost you to replace it, used, and maybe that will adjust its worth to you. It's hard to let go of things we feel have "value," but go to a thrift store and see how much you can buy of "value" for so very little, or how much the thing that cost you plenty has decreased in value. It's the ebb and flow of life and possessions. Your cast-off is someone else's bargain and treasure, and theirs, your bargain. If you keep it you are denying others their lucky find. Think of how much more use it will get at someone else's home, rather than storing it in your basement or attic while you wait to find a need for it.

You probably know what needs doing to prepare your house for sale. But if you need ideas, search "How to prepare your home to sell" online. Your house needs to be as close to perfect as possible, including cabinets and closets. It's hard! Start early, pace yourself, maybe clean out one room per week. If your decorations aren't showing off your house, then they are just taking up space and maybe need to go into storage. Only a few items on a shelf. The eye likes odd numbers and varied heights, and places for the eye to rest (space between items).

No smells! Take excellent care of litter boxes, and no strong kitchen smells. Kitchens and baths should be shiny and spotless. Another book I would highly recommend is *Speed Cleaning* by Jeff Campbell because who wants to spend time cleaning? And while the house is on the market, realtor or not, it needs to be nearly ready to show at all times. The tips in that book about top-down cleaning, easy dusting, organizing cleaning supplies and materials like diapers as rags and old toothbrushes have made cleaning easier for me for decades. I love efficiency experts who share their knowledge.

If needed, clean molding, baseboards, windows, and sills. A clean house is more appealing to any buyer.

Store clutter, toys, and boxes you've packed up in one area (maybe a corner of a basement or garage if you can't get rid of them) or put them in a storage locker, leaving rooms looking spacious. Store out-of-season clothes elsewhere if possible, like under the bed, to make closets look bigger. Donate everything you don't wear, because everyone loves big closets, and fewer clothes will make the closets look bigger. Clean off porches and patios.

Put a bucket for shower supplies under the sink, don't leave the bottles around the shower or tub. Personal care items breed like bunnies; get rid of any you don't use.

In real estate things such as light fixtures or curtain rods that are attached to your home are considered part of the real estate. Curtains are not, though people often leave them if they match the room. Mirrors above bathroom sinks stay. List flat screens attached to the wall as an exclusion in your real estate ad if you plan on taking them with you when you move. If you cherish any light fixtures or mirrors, buy inexpensive replacements and install *before* you take pictures or show the home. It might throw a monkey wrench into negotiations if your buyer is also in love with your chandelier, and then you inform them it's not included in the sale. At the very least, if you can't get it down before showing, list it as an exclusion to the sale so the buyer knows not to fall in love with it.

Once you have packed up or donated all the belongings you can afford to live without while your home is on the market, try to arrange the rooms in the most pleasing set up. Decorating can help sell a home, which is why "staging" is a growing career. Some realtors have people on staff that will do the staging for/with you. Others have leads on someone you can hire to do it for you. As a For Sale By Owner, if you have the money and feel it might help to have a decorator give you staging advice, search online for "staging a home." It shouldn't cost more than a couple hundred dollars and can make an enormous difference. They might re-arrange furniture, or suggest inexpensive purchases that will warm the place up, or punch it up with accents, like pillows. You can also look up how to stage your home yourself, or invite a friend who enjoys decorating over for coffee and ask for advice, which is what I did.

All of this fixing up goes for the outside as well. You want the first view of your home, as the buyer is driving up, to be a pleasant one. No broken items cluttering up the yard. Have it hauled away. Spruce up the yard and any planting beds. The entry to your home should be as welcoming as possible. Consider putting a fresh coat of paint on the front door or some flowers around the entry (annuals so they'll keep blooming as you sell).

For me, preparing my house for sale was the hardest part and it was *very* hard work. Again, something I had to get done *regardless or whether or not I had a realtor*. The actual work of being a For Sale By Owner is so small in comparison. And at least, since I was selling on my own, I could go at my pace, which lessened the stress. I raked the yard, re-seeded bare spots in the lawn, cleaned the weeds out of flower beds that had been getting overgrown for years, pruned bushes, swept the walkways, and power washed the decks. This took me months, but I knew the house would sell faster and for more if the yard didn't look like it needed maintenance right away. That first impression is important.

You must really assess the condition of your home and disclose any problems with it. But one way to make sure you are ready for sale is to purchase a home warranty. That's an insurance policy you can offer the buyers to protect them for a certain amount of time if something goes wrong with major parts of your home. Check with companies for pricing, but if there's any doubt about the condition of your home, this can set a buyer's mind at ease, and be a great selling point.

Another terrific option — again, if you have the funds to pay for it — is to have a preemptive house inspection done before you put the house on the market. Most buyers will want a home inspection as a contingency in the purchase and sale document, and they will arrange and pay for it. They can dissolve the contract if the inspection reveals something about the house they don't like, usually above a certain threshold of repair cost. Buyers shouldn't be able to back out of the purchase because your porch lightbulb needs replacing. A lawyer can include wording in the purchase and sale document to make sure this doesn't happen. Hiring your own inspector before you put the house up for sale can reveal any major flaws and prevent you from being surprised when the buyer's inspector comes and results in painful price re-negotiation.

For example, if I'd done this on my last house, I would have known my roof needed replacing and could have had it done before it went on the market, and maybe kept my first full-price offer. If your inspection reveals major flaws, you can decide if you want to fix them or list them as disclosures. Talk to your attorney if you have questions about things that need disclosure.

STEP THREE: HIRE A REAL ESTATE PHOTOGRAPHER, OR TAKE PICTURES

Pictures are the first look that someone gets of your home, so treat them like the very important marketing tool that they are. If you are going to do For Sale By Owner, and if you can afford it, hire an experienced real estate photographer. Once I realized that wide-angle, high-resolution pictures were best, I looked briefly into a device to buy for my phone for it to take wide-angle pictures. But for about the same money, I hired a photographer who specialized in real estate photography. He charged $199 to generate both high resolution and normal pictures, as well as a video. He took 44 pictures of both the inside and outside of the house. FYI: The video is a slideshow of the pictures. He didn't walk through the house with a video camera.

The photographer I hired for my fourth house sale was amazing, and the pictures were gorgeous. He knew the angles to take, brought special lighting with him, and was very experienced about how to present the rooms to their best advantage. He had a wide-angle lens that took in more, but the rooms didn't look warped or strange. He worked really quickly because he knew what he was doing and what would look best.

The photographer sent me the pictures by email and they were so good my son said, "Wow, I can't believe we live there!"

Because the pictures draw someone in to see your home, you want them to be great. Realtors often take home pictures themselves and can do a good job with this, or they have a photographer they use regularly. But if you're not using a realtor you can still hire a great real estate photographer pretty inexpensively. A few hundred dollars of upfront costs as a For Sale By Owner can save you thousands in commissions later.

Be careful with having pictures that look a lot nicer than the house looks in person. Some realtors use a filter that makes your pictures look like a drawing or painting, I think to minimize flaws. But though you want to draw customers to your home, if the pictures seem touched-up or taken at such a wide angle that the rooms look way bigger than they are in reality, or have a filter to hide flaws, perhaps your potential buyer's first impression will be disappointment. I've had that experience and now I look more critically at real estate pictures and try to imagine how it really looks in person. Don't misrepresent. Also, never use pictures from a previous sale that you didn't take or pay for, as you could be violating copyright.

Clean the house really well before you do pictures. Maybe mopping floors and dusting is not so critical, but hide clutter, clear off counters, and take bright pictures during the day.

Natural light looks better, so try to avoid using flash. Take the pictures before 4:00 pm. Represent your home as honestly as you can. Use landscape mode, not portrait. Bathrooms should sparkle. Turn on all the lights. Bring in extra lamps for lighting from other rooms if you need to. Take off the lampshades on lamps that are not in the picture to shed the most light in your room. Experiment with taking pictures from different angles — maybe for example, from a few steps up on a stool, or kneeling down, which can make a room look larger. Look at pictures online for ideas of what camera angles work. Some phones allow you to brighten the picture before you take it, so learn about your picture-taking device and get nice, bright, clear photos.

When you're done, check out how many pictures can go into the online ad with the service you'll be using and decide which pictures to use. You'll want at least one of the outside, the kitchen, a bath, the family or living room, and the master bedroom.

STEP FOUR: DECIDE ON A PRICE BASED ON MARKET RESEARCH OR HIRE AN APPRAISER

Your house will sell if you price it right. If it's cheaper than any other comparable home in your town, buyers will see it as a bargain and most likely it will sell quickly. On the other hand, you don't want to give away your home. The trick here is to find the right price, one that will sell your house as quickly as possible but also maximize the amount of money coming to you.

Your price needs to reflect what is on the market. "Comps" is short for "comparables," which means homes similar to yours in location, size, age, and condition. Check out your competition.

Drive by homes in your area, especially ones priced similarly. How many are on the market in that range? Supply and demand will also play a role.

There are a lot of factors to consider when pricing your home. A house comparable in every way to yours in another town might still be worth much more. Perhaps you've heard of the three most important factors in real estate pricing: "Location, location, and location." When I sold my house, there were homes in the very next town that would have sold for nearly double what I was asking for the same square footage and amenities. But my town, a small, rural town with few services couldn't compare to the neighboring town with shopping centers, community center, senior center, trash pickup, an arts center, top school district, and abundant programming for children. Some people who came to my first open houses bought in surrounding towns, rather than in my town. This is especially important for relocations, people who don't already have kids committed to a friend group or school system.

If you go on eBay, you can find products listed for all kinds of crazy prices. But if you really want to know what a product is worth, check the "sold items" box and then check what similar items *sold for.* That's the actual value of the item — what customers are actually willing to pay, not what the owner is wishing they will get. Fortunately, you can do the same research in real estate, and it's the first step in determining the listing price for your home.

Years ago, I had to go to the registry of deeds and look up specific properties to find out what they sold for. Realtors used to do this all the time to find comparable properties to use in setting pricing. With access to real estate sites online, you can search the sold listings and find out what homes in your town actually sold for.

You'll get several useful pieces of information about a home looking at the sold listings, and one of the most important (after location) is square footage. If you need to find yours, your real estate assessment will have a rough square footage calculation. Or you can measure yourself, research how to measure and calculate it. It involves multiplying the width and length of each room and adding them all up. I had my square footage from my building plans. If you built your house, you can also find the square footage on the blueprints.

The "sold" house listings will often have a price-per-square-foot figure. That's the selling price of the house divided by the square feet. This will vary quite a bit. New homes often have a higher price-per-square-foot than older ones, perhaps because people expect more costs of upkeep with an older house or they like new modern floor plans. So, if you own an antique home you can't compare it with the price-per-square-foot of the new homes in a development going in down the street, even though it's the same neighborhood and same size house. Yours will most likely be less unless you find a generous buyer who adores antique homes. You could tell a buyer that your house is "like new," because you've replaced the windows and the roof and the heating system. It's great to point those out, but really, comparing your old home to a new one is apples to oranges.

Be realistic about the condition of your home. If it needs updating or has some wear and tear, fix it or adjust the price accordingly. You may think it's not worth replacing worn, dirty carpeting when a buyer can just do so after purchase and pick out carpet to their tastes, but if the first impression of your home is yucky carpeting, it might help to sell if you put in a new carpet in a neutral color. If you don't, consider that you may take a hit on the price of the home for that — or any other glaring house fix-up projects that exist.

Most of us don't have the money to fix all the problems with the home before we sell and know that we might not get top dollar because of it.

I started coming up with a price for my home by looking at the sold listings. You could make yourself a spreadsheet for this comparison, if you like that kind of thing. To be honest, I made my notes on a napkin. I went through the sold listings for the last six months and wrote down address, price, a brief description, age, and price per square foot. It was a hot market and a lot of houses were selling, which inflated prices. I was excited! I didn't compare my home with antiques, but being ten years old, I couldn't compare to new construction either, so I was looking for homes that had been around about as long as mine. You can add any search criteria you like to browsing the sold listings (e.g., number of bedrooms, garage, etc.), just as you would when searching for a home to buy. So, if your home is an 1880's antique, search for sold homes that were built around the same time, within maybe a 50-year window, to get the most similar comparison homes and make your estimate more accurate.

My house was a large, four-bedroom home. Poking around, I came up with about 12 properties that I felt offered the best comparison to mine. Some were slightly bigger, some were newer, and none had what I thought was the best part of my house: a floor plan that was custom designed with a large family's living style and storage needs in mind. Plus, we built my house to look old, with wide wood moldings and custom horizontal five-panel doors, as well as other things that made it unique.

This is where it gets tricky. As an owner, you think your home is special. A realtor can set you right on that, but if you are selling it yourself, grow a thick skin for critiquing your home. I realized that I didn't compare with the homes in other towns that had more services to offer families, and my yard was a disaster. I did what I could to fix it up, but I knew I would take a hit because of the overgrown back yard. I gave up formal living and dining spaces for more practical use, but there will be families who want that formal entertaining space. I hoped that families would see how I used my square footage and I'd be at an advantage, but maybe not. And I looked with a critical eye at the wear and tear that ten years of family living in my home had wrought. I did the best I could to touch-up paint and clean like crazy, but doing this alone and in the middle of moving and finding a new residence meant that there was only so much I could accomplish. I had to adjust the price accordingly.

Once I'd come up with the 12 most-comparable, recently sold properties, I added up each price-per-square-foot, and divided that total by 12, giving me an average price-per-square-foot. Then I multiplied that average by my home's square footage, and this was my asking price.

Then, I looked at what was currently on the market and compared their price-per-square-foot to mine. I drove by the homes that most closely aligned with my house's size and condition. I felt like I had a good price and that the price-per-square-foot of my house was fair — or even a bit of a bargain.

When a realtor offers to do a "market analysis" for you, they will use their knowledge of real estate and the data of both recently sold properties and properties currently listed for sale to come up with an estimate of your home's asking price. They offer this to you for free, and it is done with the process I just described.

But, that is *not* the same as a real estate *appraisal*, which is a more comprehensive and professional assessment of your home's value that you pay a professional appraiser to provide for you. We hire appraisers to establish the value of a home during situations when it's important to establish the actual market value of a home, like when people get divorced, or when a bank is looking to approve a mortgage or home equity loan.

Realtors who do a market analysis for you will come to inspect your home and make an appointment to come back with it in a few days. This is when you will get the hard sell. They will tell you they did a lot of work coming up with this report, and it will be a lovely document, with pictures of the comparable properties, and pages of information about their realtor's office and what they can do to help you reach more buyers. They'll try to convince you not to do For Sale By Owner and want you to sign a contract making them your listing realtor.

Realtors will tell you that if you let them represent you, they can get you more money for your home and sell it more quickly. This has not been my experience, nor does the research support this claim. At this point please, please re-read the section in Chapter 5 "View with Caution Realtor's Advice Against For Sale By Owner" for more information on the Wisconsin study and other arguments against For Sale By Owner that a realtor might give you.

If you are more comfortable working with a realtor, that's fine. Before you sign a contract, though, know the facts about realtor vs. For Sale By Owner, and know how much money it will cost you.

When I was getting ready to sell, I had two realtors who insisted on giving me a free market analysis of my home. When they present the market analysis it's difficult to tell them, "Thank you very much, but I still don't want to hire you." Be prepared to say, "No thanks," or at the very least, "Let me think about it" when they come over with the market analysis if you are planning to try For Sale By Owner first. I'd suggest doing your own research. It doesn't take long, you can be very accurate, and you won't be obligated to anyone. And, it's a smart exercise so you can compare what you discover with what a realtor offers you as a selling price. You can also compare your asking price with what the real estate sites estimate is the value of the home.

Some realtors now try a strategy of listing well below market in order to start a bidding war. This seems risky and more in line with the realtor's goals than the homeowner's. As a For Sale By Owner, price realistically. I'd be careful about listing too far below market to create a bidding war. At the right price, a house will sell. If it goes for less than you expected, you may walk away feeling disappointed, like you gave your house away. If you do your own research and are realistic about the condition and location of your home, and make sure there aren't houses as nice as yours priced lower in your town, you can feel confident that the price you picked is fair. There remains the squishy goal of finding the right buyer, because price is only one factor, buying a home is a very personal decision. Someone has to want to live in your home and make it theirs. I hope you find someone who thinks your house is unique and wonderful and the perfect place for them to live.

If you're willing to pay for it, you can hire a real estate appraiser to determine the market price of your home. Banks hire them to make sure that the loan amount on a home is not more than the bank could sell the home for if the home were to go into foreclosure, so they are experts at determining a true and accurate market value. The market appraisal is more detailed than a real estate agent's market analysis. If you hire an appraiser, make sure you point out unusual features that might not be self-evident (like 2x6 construction) and any upgrades you've made. Though costly, an official appraisal will make sure you price your home correctly, and copies of it are an excellent marketing tool you can present to potential buyers, making them comfortable with your asking price. If you don't mind spending the money to have it done, this is the best option for pricing your home, but you can still get a good idea by doing your own research the same way the realtors do, as I explained above.

Take into account that when you list your home, you'll decide what, if anything, you will pay realtors who bring a buyer (or buyers who bring their realtors). And, the new real estate commissions laws require that the amount the seller is offering to buyer's agents is not listed in the MLS. If you sell to someone who has a realtor, you'll may decide to pay the fee (as a percentage of selling price). If you decide you don't want to pay the co-broke fee and put 0% in your listing, the realtor may walk away, telling the buyer, "You're on your own with this one," or, they may have had the buyer sign a contract stating that the buyer will be responsible for their fee if the seller doesn't pay. The percentage you offer doesn't have to be the full 2.5 or 3.0%; you can offer whatever you like. I made a mistake in thinking that realtors would ignore the fact that I was a For Sale By Owner and work with me, bringing me buyers, as long as I offered the same commission they would make on any other sale. The reality is realtors aren't thrilled with For Sale By Owners because it's bad for their business overall. If they are working with a client who sees your home online, though, they *will* work with you as long as you will pay them, or they know their clients will pay them. You can put in 0% and then have a conversation with a realtor if they call with a ready buyer. I had friends who told all realtors, "We'll pay you 1%," to which some realtors walked away, while others brought their clients. Or, you can have them come see the home, and when the offer comes in, with a realtor's fee as part of it, you can decide to negotiate or not, depending on how good the offer is. If you only willing to pay a small percentage to realtors, or none at all, you may be willing to price your house below market price to sell quickly, essentially passing some of your savings on commission to your buyer.

Finally, if you grossly overprice your house, even if you find a buyer who agrees to pay the asking price, the bank's real estate appraisal may prevent the buyer from getting a loan to cover the purchase. In the case of a foreclosure, the bank doesn't want to end up with a property that they can't sell for enough to cover the loan.

STEP FIVE: PREPARE MARKETING MATERIALS

Once you have your pictures and a price, you can put together an ad. You'll want to buy a yard sign. Local home stores have ready-made ones, or check online for custom ones that provide a weatherproof space for brochures. You'll want a sign because neighbors might want to move, or have their friends or relatives move to the neighborhood, and a yard sign will alert them that you are selling. I would advise that the sign say "For Sale by Owner," so they know they won't need a realtor to make the sale.

You'll also need at least one "Open House" sign so buyers can easily find your open house when you have it.

I put together a brochure easily on Canva, a free online tool for creating all kinds of materials that has lots of snazzy templates. You can do this, too. Just gather some of your pictures, a floor plan if you have one, the price, and contact information. Use more pictures than words, maybe bullet points of features to make for easy reading. List a description of the house, any improvements or special features, the neighborhood's or town's highlights, schools, shopping, and amenities. Don't make people call you for the price and update your flyers if the price changes. Include your contact information. Include that you are For Sale By Owner and are happy to work directly with buyers, that you have a lawyer ready to handle the sale, and will work with agents who bring a buyer (if you will) and what percentage you will pay. Perhaps something to the effect that: "Once we agree on a price, my attorney will write up a sales contract which you can then take to your attorney or bank. Deposits will be held in escrow." This way they know you are working with a professional and that you will let their professionals see and approve of any contracts between the two parties. If making a brochure feels like a lot, you can print out a few pages of your online listing to give to potential buyers. That was all I did for my early house sales. Dropping off a copy of the brochure to your neighbors might help you find a sale through someone who wants family or friends to move nearby.

Print enough brochures (color if possible) to put several in your sign (if it has a place to hold them) and print some more to give people who come to open houses. Having something that buyers can take with them gives them some information to reference and will remind them of your house details.

I used a generic For Sale By Owner sign and made a one-page flyer for open houses, which took about 10 minutes to create. I had copies of a floor plan that I printed for open houses, and a list of features. None of this was overwhelming or time-consuming. In a seller's market, you might not even find it necessary.

Though I don't like any kind of high-pressure sales and don't think it works on a house, it may be handy to collect email addresses of buyers who visit your home in case you drop the price and want to let interested buyers know. A house is such a personal decision; the best you can do is write your ad to evoke the emotion of a happy home, get the house clean and free of personal items, and allow buyers time to view your home without pressure. But when I started, if I had collected contact information from people who liked my home at $648,000, maybe they would love it at $628,000. If they had liked or saved the listing online, they should receive a notice when I adjust the price. But you never know, and it wouldn't hurt to put out a piece of paper and tell people that if they want updates on the home, they can leave their contact information. Most buyers are used to doing so because realtors collect contact information at open houses, hoping to gain them as a client.

If you are providing either a home warranty or did your own home inspection and have that report, have that information and copies of the paperwork at the open house. If you made a spreadsheet of recent sales with price-per-square-foot calculations and your house compares favorably, you can also provide that information for the buyers. Likewise, if you paid for a market appraisal, provide a copy of that to prospective buyers.

STEP SIX: LIST YOUR HOUSE ONLINE AS FOR SALE BY OWNER

When you get ready to list your home online, start by assembling all the components you need. Create a file where you can write the description of your house, and keep your digital photos on your computer. You might edit the house description occasionally. Use the file and cut and paste from it as a backup, do your edits in there, not online. Proofread, spell, and grammar check the description. Have all your pictures backed up. This will make entering an ad into online sites easier and will help if you will list in more than one place.

Sometimes there are glitches in entering data, so having it in a file on your computer keeps you from losing any work. Pictures should be ones you took yourself or hired a photographer to do. Don't use photos from previous listings of your house (it may violate copyright). Write down all the dimensions of your rooms and make a list of features you want to highlight. Put in captions for your photos, if that's an option. Photo captions can be kept in your house description file, and are another opportunity to communicate to the buyer. Use vibrant language and highlight features, don't just label with room names. For example, instead of labeling a picture "Family Room," you could instead fit in a more colorful description, like, "Expansive Sunken Gathering Room with plenty of space for Entertaining Guests." If you have time, check other house listings for ideas.

In Chapter Four I wrote about how to write a description that brings you buyers, and how the final version of my online ad's home description increased my attendance at open houses that weekend, bringing me a full-price offer. The two most important things I think you can do to sell your home are to price it right and then write it right. You need to price your home appropriately for the market. And then, you need to write a description that isn't merely a cold recital of the features of the home, but an ad that evokes emotion and a vision of how great it is to live there. See the previous chapter if you need ideas on how to accomplish this, and check out ads for houses online to get more ideas about how to write a truly compelling house description. It's an important part of advertising. Gone are the days when you had to advertise with "3BR RNCH, GAR, .25AC" (three-bedroom ranch, garage, on 1/4 acre). Use your words! Find out how many are allowed in the description section of the online site you are using, and use every single character. Fill it up with feeling words.

Once you have all your information together, follow directions to post your ad in the online site of your choice. It's straightforward, if tedious and time consuming. If you have all your measurements and photos ready to go, it will go more quickly.

Zillow.com is currently ranked highest with the most visitors, but you can also list on Trulia.com, Craigslist.com, Facebook marketplace, Yahoo.com, Fsbo.com, Forsalebyowner.com, eBay, and Realtor.com. Research where to place For Sale By Owner real estate ads for more ideas and up-to-date information on what sites get the most traffic when you are ready to list. I'm certain things will continue to evolve in real estate sales, and new venues for listings may make their way onto the scene after I publish this book.

When I listed my last house, I didn't get referrals through my flat-fee listing broker, ever, and when, as a test, my friend called on my listing, they discouraged her from contacting me. Please read more about this in Chapter Five, "Avoid the Flat Fee Broker and the MLS (Important!)." I had been recommending starting with Zillow.com or one of the other real estate websites as a For Sale By Owner listing, free on Zillow, and they display that you are For Sale By Owner, which is key, and people can even search for "For Sale By Owner" if they are looking to save money buying. However, Zillow has since moved their FSBO listings to a separate tab, and because of that, I'd recommend doing a flat fee listing, or start as an FSBO listing and change it if you get few or no calls on your ad.

I had a friend who recently listed with ForSaleByOwner.com, and they were able, through that site, to list both in the MLS and on Zillow.com as a clearly identified For Sale By Owner ad. They got numerous offers, many from buyers who came with their realtors (perhaps these buyers saw the ads on Realtor.com and didn't know it was a For Sale By Owner). In the end, they chose to accept the offer of a buyer who came without a realtor, as the bottom line was that they kept more of their equity by doing so. If you absolutely want to list in the MLS, at least see if there is a way to list on other sites as a For Sale By Owner. That way you may be able to avoid having to pay the buyer's realtor's fees.

Another important thing you need to be aware of is that wherever you list there will be realtors advertising on your page, and it will appear as if they are the listing brokers. When friends of mine were selling their house, they put their ad up on Zillow as a For Sale By Owner and asked me to look at the ad. Their contact information was below all the realtors who had paid to advertise on their house listing! This is a problem. If I was a buyer, I would probably just call the top realtor, assuming that that was the listing realtor. So I suggested my friends put as the first line in their ad, right in the description: "We are For Sale By Owner and happy to work directly with buyers! Please contact us at: (555) 555-5555," so that people didn't contact any of the realtors first. You should *also* put your contact information right in the space that reads "What I Love About This Property," as that's another space where you can tell owners you are For Sale By Owner, and at the time of this printing the space it occupies is just above all the realtor's ads. I'd love to see the real estate sites come up with an option for paying for a For Sale By Owner listing (right now it's free), one where you can be the first or the only contact on your home's listing page.

If a realtor brings you a buyer, it entitles them to the co-broke fee, if you've offered one, and it might be as simple as the buyer calling a realtor advertising on your page first, instead of calling you. So, make it easy and obvious for them to skip the realtors and go directly to you, by putting your contact information right in the ad. You hope to save money for yourself, but you can also cut a better deal with a buyer if you aren't paying any real estate commission, which gives you more bargaining room to sell more quickly. It doesn't matter if you sell for a little less when you compare it with selling for more but having to pay commissions and ending up with less net money in your pocket. Being FSBO gives you lots more negotiating room.

I also advised my friends to offer a lower commission. And you, as a seller, aren't required to offer anything (0%) if you don't want to pay a realtor, ever. My suggestion to my friends was to put in a 1% or a 1.5% co-broke fee, which based on the price of the home, would be around $3000, which seems reasonable for showing the house and drawing up an offer letter. Realtors can't see what you are offering, and will need to call you if their clients want to see the house. If a realtor comes to you with a buyer, perhaps one that had signed a buyer-broker contract, the buyer could compensate that realtor.

Once your ad goes live, have a friend contact you from your listing, testing that buyers can reach you easily and that emails are not ending up in your spam folder.

Decide for yourself if you are comfortable using your own contact information. I bought a temporary phone with its own number, but since I put my ad in MLS and I didn't get contacted that way, it was a waste of money (my house sold through an open house). But if you are putting a number directly into your ad (which MLS does not allow you to do), you might think about whether or not you want to use your personal cell or email address.

STEP SEVEN: SCHEDULE OPEN HOUSES ON THE WEEKENDS BY THURSDAY OF EACH WEEK

After making sure that people can reach you easily from your ad, your next step is to make it easy for people to see your home. Most people will search the online ads all week, but might make definite plans about which homes to visit by the end of the week. Put a notice in for your open house by Thursday to give people time to put you on their list when they are making their weekend open house real estate shopping plans. This change of adding an open house to your online ad (which you can edit anytime you want) will send a notice out to anyone who has saved your home as one of interest.

Realtors have brief open houses as much to gather new clients as to show off a house for sale. But your open houses can last as long as you will hang around the house waiting for people to arrive. Realtors tend to have their open houses around the same hours: maybe 10-12:00 or 12-2:00. But yours can last until 4:00, or 6:00, after all the other open houses are over, and perhaps you'll get more buyers to swing by if you are available for these unusual times. If you can, while your home is on the market, schedule an open house every week. People need to browse, sometimes more than once. Whether a home is right for them is a personal decision, and it's a big, expensive decision, too. Give them time to mull your house over.

Hosting an open house may feel hard if you are an introvert, and I'm a little shy, but I found it delightful. Often, people are out looking at houses, not to buy, but for decorating ideas or just for fun. That's okay, as long as you are also there to welcome serious buyers. Though realtors will say they will only bring qualified, interested buyers to your home, nobody controls who goes to open houses. Have patience and welcome anyone, regardless.

I never gave tours of my house. I put valuables away, or stored them off-site, or locked them in my car. Then I allowed people to roam the house at their leisure, which is the same thing that happens at every realtor's open house I've ever attended. The realtor didn't accompany or chaperone me through any open house I've ever been to; I signed in with the realtor and then did my own tour. I think people need the time and space to evaluate a home for themselves, and I was comfortable letting them do so. If I attended an open house hosted by a For Sale By Owner and then they followed me around pointing out all the features, it would feel like a hard sell to me, and that would make me uncomfortable. But do what works for/feels comfortable for you. I gave visitors the brochure with a floor plan and invited them to "show yourselves around, take your time, let me know if you have questions." I wanted to convey to buyers that I would be an easy, reasonable person to negotiate with.

If a buyer comes with a realtor, you can decide whether you'd like to accompany them on the tour. You might want to in case the realtor tries to point out anything negative about your home, or is pushing a different home to the buyer.

If you allow a realtor to bring buyers to your home for a tour, call them later to get feedback, especially if it didn't result in a sale. It might give you information you can use for fixing something that buyers are concerned about, or perhaps indicate that a price adjustment is necessary.

Prepare for the open house by making everything sparkly clean and clear of clutter. And truly, I don't want to minimize how hard it is to live like this, especially if you have kids. I recommend the book *Speed Cleaning* by Jeff Campbell to help keep things in tip-top shape. Maybe water the lawn on the morning of the open house, mow the day before. Clear countertops in the kitchen and stow bathroom clutter. Stash all family photos and paperwork. On the day of the open house, set the temperature to cool in the summer, warm in the winter, making it as comfortable and welcoming as possible, including a welcome mat at the door. Potted flowers by the front door are a welcoming touch. I set an outdoor table with flowers in a glass (from my yard), candles ready to be lit, a water pitcher and glasses, and pillows on the chairs. I put a few pool toys in the pool, arranged deck chairs with towels. Sometimes I just sat out there with a book while people toured the house. Have pets and children out of the home if possible, because again, it's hard for a buyer to envision it as their home if your family is clearly inhabiting it. While selling, attempt to organize your belongings in such a way as to make it easy to clear off counters and spruce up the home quickly. I kept a lot of things in baskets while I was selling, which meant I could take the baskets off the kitchen counter and store them neatly in the pantry for showings.

If you have wood, tile, or laminate floors, a wide dust mop

can get your home tidy fast. Plastic buckets can stow shower supplies under a sink and make your shower look tidy. Turn on all lights. Though this seems wasteful during the day, it can make your home feel more welcoming.

No one could inspect inside my car, but nothing inside the house was off-limits, so I often made good use of laundry baskets to take paperwork, clutter, laundry-in-progress, and sometimes even dirty dishes out of the house into the car, so my countertops, office area, laundry room, and mudrooms looked much better! It's a super fast way to spruce up the house.

Put away toys or personal belongings you (or your children) would be horrified to have other children touch. It's hard to control how other people, especially children, will behave in your home, so protect your belongings before the open house.

When I was selling, I purposely put out some of my kid's toys from when they were younger in the family room, some indestructible wooden trains. I figured it might help buy some time for people with kids who were sick and tired of looking at homes if the kids could play for a bit.

Neatly display printable sale materials on the counter: listing sheet or brochure, lists of special features or improvements to the house (often helpful if you are comparing to new construction), floor plans or landscape plans, school system stats or other information about the town, information about conservation land, parks, shopping, restaurants, homeowner's association information, warranties, inspection reports, and blank offer letters provided by your attorney.

None of this is necessary, but it's another opportunity to communicate marketing information to the buyer and sell not just the home but the area and the town. You're the expert. You know what's good in the neighborhood; you know the availability of restaurants or hiking trails or proximity to services.

Be ready with an introduction about your house. Write it down if you want to remember everything. Mention that you are For Sale By Owner, willing to work directly with buyers and your attorney will prepare contracts and hold deposits held in escrow. Offer everyone information on how to make an offer (print off blank offer forms). "Our lawyer can help walk you through the process," is a great way to help set a buyer at ease.

You don't have to use a lawyer for your home sale. I recommend it because it reassures me I am doing everything correctly, but offer letters and purchase and sale template contracts are available online. If you and your buyer are comfortable not using a lawyer, that's fine. But if you are new to For Sale By Owner and feel nervous about not using a realtor, hiring a lawyer (for a fraction of a real estate commission) can help smooth out the process and make you feel more confident in your ability to sell your home on your own.

You can also have a sign-in sheet for contact info.

It's important for you to be available to buyers when they'd like to see the home, and by all means show the home as soon as possible when a potential buyer calls. But your next best tool for selling For Sale By Owner is regular open houses. I shared responsibility for them with my ex-husband; he took one day per weekend, and I took the other, but we could also have had one open house per weekend and alternated weekends.

Make sure people can find the house easily. If you have special directions, put them right in your ad when you schedule the open house.

Though realtors have open houses regularly and are usually at the house alone, if you don't have a significant other with you, consider asking a friend to keep you company if that makes you feel more comfortable.

You will get people who are just curious about your house with no intention to buy, but don't let that discourage you. People do this all the time, it's entertaining. And even if they aren't buying, maybe they'll pass along the information to someone who is. All my sales have happened because of an open house. For a For Sale By Owner, I think open houses are a critical selling tool.

STEP EIGHT: SUBMIT OFFERS AND EARNEST MONEY TO YOUR ATTORNEY FOR ESCROW, SIGN P&S

When a potential buyer contacts you, return all correspondence and calls promptly. If they would like to make an offer, give them your offer form and specify what you would like as earnest money deposit. They should submit offers with earnest money in the form of a check made out to your attorney's escrow account. You don't cash the check yourself and put it in your own account. Your attorney will handle keeping the buyer's deposit in an account for you until closing. Your attorney can also provide you with a standard offer form, which will indicate the price offered for the home and that the offer is contingent on a satisfactory purchase and sale document drawn up and signed by both parties.

Your lawyer can take care of preparing the purchase and sale document (P&S) for you, or if you had a buyer who is working with a real estate attorney or realtor, they might deliver the purchase and sale for you and your attorney to review. You should make sure your attorney reviews this document on your behalf before you sign it. Ask your attorney to keep deadlines tight; if this deal falls through, you want to get your home back on the market as soon as possible. So, for example, specify the timeframe in which the house inspection will happen so you don't wait weeks and then have the deal fall apart because of something found during the inspection. That's valuable time that you could have continued to market your home.

Your attorney will then prepare any other items required for closing, working with the seller's attorney or their bank's attorney. The bank's attorney may be the only attorney working on the buyer's behalf, as their interests are aligned. Closing can take place at an attorney's office or, sometimes, the registry of deeds.

Once your home is under agreement, you can put "Pending Offer" up on your online ad. But don't stop showing your home if you're contacted by a different potential buyer who wants to see it. Let them know if there's an offer on the table, or if it's under agreement with a purchase and sale signed by both parties. You never know what will happen with the original offer, and if you've read this entire book, you've seen how a deal can fall through, and how valuable a back-up buyer or offer can be.

Don't get mad or insulted through the process. Counter every offer and do it in writing, as quickly as you can. If your attorney acts as the go-between, that might help keep emotions out of it. Explain your reason for countering (the market research you did on comparable properties, or special features). Don't interpret a lowball offer as an insult. Don't get involved in an argument and stay calm, even if your buyer is not. Keep details on negotiations and agreements confidential and never discuss anyone's personal financial information. Not only is this considerate, you never know who knows who and what might affect your deal.

STEP NINE: SCHEDULE AN INSPECTION AND WALK-THROUGH OF YOUR HOUSE

If it's a desirable property or a seller's market, some buyers might forgo a house inspection to have their offer accepted. But usually, the end of the process involves allowing for the buyer to bring an inspector to your home, which is a very common contingency in the purchase and sale. This means that if something comes up during an inspection that bothers the buyer, they can back out of the deal. My lawyer put in a minimum cost for this inspection contingency. In other words, if a repair would cost under a certain amount, we could fix it or offer an allowance for the buyer to fix it, but only repairs over this threshold amount would be a valid reason for nullifying the contract. Have your lawyer add a similar threshold to your purchase and sale, you don't want a buyer to walk away for a minor or cosmetic issue, especially since you've now lost some time marketing the home. If there are more expensive problems that need repairs, then you'll re-negotiate after the inspection if the buyer is still willing to buy the home.

When my buyers brought the inspector to the home, I stayed out of the way but told them I was available for questions. It is the inspector's job to find anything that's wrong with your house, and it's hard to listen to them talk about problems or potential problems. Better to let them have their time at the house and address problems when they share the inspection report with you. Hopefully, you'll have the chance to put their mind at ease about anything negative that shows up in the report.

STEP TEN: PREPARE FOR AND ATTEND CLOSING

Closing can take place right at the registry of deeds, and in that case, the deed can be recorded right away and you may be able to walk out with your check. Or, it could happen at an attorney's office or at another mutually agreed-upon location. If your attorney schedules the closing, make it a convenient location for you. You won't get your money until they record the deed, and you might be able to wait until that happens at the registry if the closing takes place there. Your attorney will explain this entire process to you.

If you aren't interested in attending the closing, you can grant your lawyer power of attorney and have them sign for you, and you can pick up your check later. But I've found the day of closing can bring its own surprises, and it's not over till it's over, so at least make sure you are reachable by phone when closing is taking place. You can also ask for them to wire your money to your bank.

There may be documents that you need to provide for closing — for example, a fire certificate (this is where the fire department comes to inspect your house and smoke detectors), or a condo 6D document. Ask your lawyer about anything you need to do to prepare for closing, with a timeline of when to request. For example, the fire certificate times out after a certain number of months, so if closing is delayed, you want to wait to get it until you are closer to closing. Where I live, we are required to provide a septic certificate (Title 5), which takes some time to schedule.

On the day of closing, or perhaps the day before, there's usually a walk-through inspection of the home for the buyers. This is an opportunity for the buyers to take a last look at the home, make sure that there has been no damage since the house inspection, ensure that you have removed all personal belongings, and that you made agreed-upon repairs. The home should be "broom-clean," meaning, deliver it clean. If the buyers find problems at the walk-though, you might need to negotiate at closing how to resolve the issue. In my case, there was an extraordinary amount of rainfall the night before, and a leak appeared in the basement wall. As a result, at closing, we agreed to put aside money for a repair (both the buyers and myself had called several repair places on the way to closing for a quick estimate). That money went into an escrow account and once the buyers had the leak repaired, the buyer's attorney refunded me the balance in the account.

AFTERWORD

REAL ESTATE IS CHANGING

I believe the nature of real estate is changing. The younger generation is open to new ways of doing things, changing how they drive places (Uber), get music (Spotify) or vacation (Airbnb). Real estate is no exception. For years, I was the only person I was aware of who did For Sale By Owner, but now I've met two younger couples who sold (and bought) their homes For Sale By Owner, and while writing this book I've offered advice to five more friends who bought or sold homes without a realtor. As online real estate sites displace the Multiple Listing Service (MLS) as the preferred way to search current inventory, selling a home yourself is both easier and more acceptable. And with the new real estate commissions rules, buyers might also be jumping on the real estate without realtors way of buying a home.

TESTING THE WATERS AS A FOR SALE BY OWNER

I hope my advice is helpful and that this book has given you information you can use to save money buying or selling your home. If you read all of it and decide it's too complicated, I understand. I had a real estate class in college, and I've always had an interest in it, so the details didn't feel overwhelming to me, just a curious challenge. The jargon alone presents a steep learning curve and is the reason I recommend hiring a lawyer to help you if you want to forgo the use of a realtor. Even though I had a lot of interest in real estate, I still wasn't familiar with everything. It always feels intimidating to do For Sale By Owner. But time after time I tried it, because the fact is — and I think this goes for many people — I couldn't afford to have somebody else walk away with those commissions. It's almost a hidden fee because you are paying out of house equity, but in reality, when would you, without thinking, write a check for tens of thousands of dollars for any professional service? Sellers are better off keeping that money in their pocket, to put towards their future housing purchases or whatever they want the money for.

When I add up only the hours doing the marketing to sell my home For Sale By Owner, I'd say it was about 20 hours total, 30 tops. This included getting the pictures done, writing up the ad and submitting them to online sites, hosting open houses, fielding phone calls from buyers, realtors, and my lawyer. The bulk of my hours were cleaning and tidying to get ready to sell, and that would need doing even if I had hired a realtor. The 20 hours I spent saved me about $18,000 in real estate commissions, or $900 per hour, which was the most money I'd ever made per hour!

If you're nervous about doing this, remember that you can

always list later with a realtor. Depending on how much you stand to save, it might be worth a try to do For Sale By Owner for a few weeks or months. Realtors might give you warnings about your property "going stale" but either people want to see your property or they don't. With online tools, prospective buyers have the opportunity to look closely at your home and make up their own minds. Your home needs to be priced right, whether you list with or without a realtor. If you do your research into sales in your area and you are realistic, you'll be able to price correctly, and homes sell at the right price — which doesn't necessarily mean the price you hoped to get, but the right price for the market at the current time, and in your location. I don't think I could have sold any of my homes for more money had I used a realtor. The market dictates the price, and it did, effectively.

FEEDBACK

If you could be so kind as to leave a review (or stars!) on whatever platform you found this book, I would very much appreciate it. Ratings and reviews are critically helpful for the self-published author, as are recommendations to other readers. Thanks in advance!

I wrote this book quickly, but the beauty of self-publishing is that it is relatively easy to change and update the document. So please inform me of any typos or problems, and I'll do my best to improve the book for the good of future readers. I'd be happy to add in any tips other For Sale By Owner folks have that would help people. We For Sale By Owners are a friendly lot who like to support each other. We're proud of what we've accomplished and eager to help others find the same success. I look forward to hearing if you have stories you'd like to share with me, or with others.

GOOD LUCK!

Finally, if you are buying, I hope you find *home:* everything warm, wonderful and sheltering that that word implies. One that brings you joy; a special place for relaxing on Sunday mornings with a dozen donuts.

And sellers: all the luck in the world to you. If you choose to try For Sale By Owner, I hope you are successful and this brings you increased financial freedom to finance your dreams, including the dream of your next exciting and nurturing place to live.

Home.

THANKS

Thanks to all who have helped me to proofread this book: Lisa Clemetson, Sue Hastings, Steve and Rhonda Hawthorne, Therese Keohane, Beth Logan, Laura Fedolfi, and Sue Landsman. I'm so happy for those of you who were successful at your first home sale by owner!

Special thanks to Rick Conti, who did an amazing proofread, suggested how to break it up logically and encouraged me to cut the places where readers would fall asleep. Apologies to those who read the early versions for all those the involuntary naps.

I couldn't be more grateful and astonished at the powerful editing skill of Jan Power of Power Assist.

Aleta Manugian is the real estate lawyer who made this easy for me. She was patient, kind, knowledgeable and curious. I swear she enjoyed my sales as much as I did. A great lawyer, but I daresay a better teacher because she always guided me in a way that empowered me.

Many thanks to the great writers and friends in SIPA, the

Society of Independent Publishers and Authors, for support, encouragement, and generously shared knowledge, for commiserating on the sometimes dull and boring work of writing and self-publishing, and for the warm connection we cemented during quarantine (and thank you, Zoom). And to Laura Fedolfi for creating and facilitating the SIPA group, and even more for her amazing friendship.

ABOUT THE AUTHOR

Donna Rucinski was a software engineer, a robotics and computer science teacher, and currently works in a school as a yoga and mindfulness teacher. Though she never became a realtor, she has had a lifetime of experience navigating both buying real estate without a realtor and selling as a For Sale By Owner.

Along the way she's pursued her avocation, writing. This is her first non-fiction book, but please check out her other work for middle school readers. There are YA novels coming soon, and books for grown-ups, too.

You can get information about her other books on her Facebook author page.

Made in United States
North Haven, CT
10 November 2026

22091361R00104